GREEK PASSENGER LINERS

GREEK PASSENGER LINERS

WILLIAM H. MILLER

The History Press

For Arthur Crook
Invaluable Resource, Keen Maritime Historian
& Dear Friend

Frontispiece: The Greek Line flagship *Olympia*, departing from New York in 1958 and as seen from the stern of the liner *United States*. *(Gillespie-Faber Collection)*

First published 2006
Reprinted 2017

The History Press
The Mill, Brimscombe Port,
Stroud, Gloucestershire, GL5 2QG
www.thehistorypress.co.uk

British Library Cataloguing in Publication Data.
A catalogue record for this book is available from the British Library.

ISBN 978 0 7524 3886 3

Typesetting and origination by Tempus Publishing Limited
Printed and bound by Berforts Ltd, England.

CONTENTS

FOREWORD

Together, Bill Miller and I were aboard an historic voyage: the sixtieth anniversary of the *Britanis* in July 1992. A splendid and special ship in every way, a true 'ocean liner', I was very proud to be that great ship's master at the time. The Steamship Historical Society of America had a group of 200 onboard and there were lectures, exhibits and special parties to mark the occasion. Dimitri Kaparis, the brilliant manager of special projects and new builds for Chandris since 1960, joined us. Myself, I was proud to be made a member of the Historical Society.

In this, his latest book, Bill pays tribute to many Greek passenger ships of the past half-century. It is a fascinating fleet, including such vessels as the *Olympia, Queen Frederica, Semiramis, Australis, Golden Odyssey, Dolphin IV* and, of course, my favorite, the *Britanis*. I will always have a special bond with that enduring 'steamer'. She was a classic!

As a boy, I dreamed of traveling the world and so decided to go to sea. I joined Chandris Lines in 1969 and served aboard many of their renowned passenger ships: the *Ellinis, Victoria, Australis, Regina Magna, Regina Prima* and *Amerikanis*. Chandris, or Celebrity Cruises as it is today, was possibly the greatest of all Greek passenger ship operators. Certainly it was the greatest training ground for young officers. All masters and crew actually called it 'Chandris University', a sea-going school.

I was assigned as master to the *Britanis* in 1990 and proudly stayed with her for four years. During the Second World War, when my father was serving with the US Navy and his ship was attacked, he was heroically rescued by the big American troopship, the USS *Monterey*, the same 1932-built ship that became the *Britanis* in 1970. In the end, in October 2000, I was especially saddened when we heard the news that the then sixty-eight-year-old liner sank off South Africa while under tow and on her way to the scrappers in India. To me, it was her 'suicide'. She preferred to go to the bottom of the sea.

As I write this, Bill and I are together for another special event: the maiden transatlantic crossing of the brand new, 91,000-ton *Constellation*. It is an occasion in which we look to the future, but also glance to the past, to those glorious Greek passenger ships of bygone years. I am therefore both proud and pleased to be included in this, Bill's latest book; a celebration entitled *Greek Passenger Ships*.

Captain Ioannis Papanikolaou
Master, GTS *Constellation*
November 2002

ACKNOWLEDGEMENTS

I recall sitting in the chief purser's rather cramped office onboard the Chandris *Romanza*. It was July 1990 and we were on an Eastern Mediterranean cruise out of Venice. I was then compiling a book on the great Chandris passenger lines. The ever-helpful purser had organized interviews with other officers and so I spent the entire afternoon talking of ships, their operations and sometimes about those who manned and sailed them. A thick notebook was always in hand as well as extra pens. Fortified by strong Greek coffee, it could not have been more fun or more interesting. Some of the anecdotes are included in this book.

Since then, and for this work, I have had many assistants and so my warmest thanks to each of them. I am especially grateful to the brilliant Arthur Crook for both inspiring and enlivening this title. Richard Faber is a first class assistant, especially for providing so many resource materials. And special thanks to Abe Michaelson, my business partner, who keeps meticulous records and despatches books just about everywhere.

I would also like to acknowledge the superb support and assistance of Ernest Arroyo, Frank O. Braynard, Philippe Brebant, Stephen Card, Michael Cassar, Tom Cassidy, Anthony Cooke, Luis Miguel Correia, the late Frank Cronican, the late John Gillespie, Clive Harvey, Brad Hatry, Andy Hernandez, Dimitri Kaparis, Arnold Kludas, Norman Knebel, Peter Knego, Michael D. J. Lennon, Carl Netherland-Brown, Hisashi Noma, Selim San, Sal Scannella, Antonio Scrimali, Don Stoltenberg and the late Everett Viez.

Other materials, photographs, anecdotes and insights came from the likes of Hugh Alderton, Arne Egelind, Captain Helge Brudvik, Captain Dimitrios Chilas, Tom Chirby, George Devol, Frank Duffy, the late Alex Duncan, Maurizio Eliseo, John Ferguson, Alan Goldfinger, Harry Haralambopoulos, Hans Hoffman, Shelagh Ingledow, F. Leonard Jackson, Captain Apostales Kanaris, Alex Keusseoglou, the late Andrew Kostantinides, Captain Nikos Koufoyiannis, Captain Angelo Kouris, Bino Lottero, Giuseppe Lovece, Frank Manwell, Captain Hans Mateboer, Gregory Maxwell, Rolf Meinecke, the late Vincent Messina, Captain Evgenios Misailides, Nikitas Nomikos, Captain George Panagiotakis, Robert Pelletier, Paolo Piccione, Andres & Georges Potomianos, Mario Pulice, Fred Rodriguez, Rich Romano, Jurgen Saupe, the late Victor Scrivens, Der Scutt, James Shaw, Roger Sherlock, John Sherwood, Captain Kjell Smitterberg, R. Starcevich, Norbert Swenson, Steven L. Tacey, Captain A. I. Tzamitzis, Captain Tassos Varsamis, Steffen Weirauch, Richard Weiss, James Wheeler, Albert Wilhelmi, and V.H. Young & L.A. Sawyer.

INTRODUCTION

When I was still a schoolboy, back in the late 1950s, and reading (and re-reading) that first edition of Laurence Dunn's superb *Passenger Liners*, the Greek passenger ship fleet had not quite come into its own. At that time the Greek Line had the biggest ships, beginning with the *Olympia*, said to be the national flagship even if she was actually under the Liberian flag, and moving on to the likes of the *New York* and the *Arkadia*. There was also the very popular *Queen Frederica*, run by the National Hellenic American Line, an arm of the immensely successful Home Lines. Otherwise, companies such as Chandris were just beginning (with the secondhand *Patris*, which was making its first trips out to Melbourne and Sydney for the so-called Europe–Australia Line, a name soon dropped). Then, there was only a small cluster of 'cruise ships' working the Aegean. Epirotiki's tiny *Semiramis* was said to have made the very first Greek islands cruise from Piraeus in 1955, but soon afterward, what an enormous fleet emerged!

While the Greek Line later expanded with the *Queen Anna Maria*, the likes of Chandris, and their sister company Chandris Cruises, seemed to burst with ship after ship, all of them bought from other owners and then usually greatly rebuilt. By 1965, their 33,500-ton, 2,200-passenger *Australis*, the former *America*, was the largest liner yet to fly the Greek colors. Other well known ships such as the *Lurline, Caronia, Stratheden, President Roosevelt, Aurelia, Aureol* and *Zion* also became Greek-owned ships. In fact, the collection soon became rather mind-boggling. There were further name changes, massive rebuilds and modernizing, life-extending refits that made my notebook records all the more involved and, all the more confusing. But then information coming out of Greece itself was sometimes unclear, uncertain. A particular ship might be reported as being scrapped, but in fact lingered on, often in some backwater anchorage, for several more years. Another might have been reported to have been sold to Greek buyers, but in fact went elsewhere. Or another was said to have been sold and renamed, but the transaction would fail, like a faulty wire, and that very ship would reappear in the following year's sailing schedule under her original name. The Greeks certainly had their mysteries – maritime mysteries.

Epirotiki Lines, for example, grew along with the likes of Efthymiadis and Typaldos, and then there were the intriguing passenger fleets of the Sun Line, Olympic Cruises, and Kavounides-K Lines Cruises. Later, by the 1970s, and as the eastern Mediterranean tourist business blossomed yet further, there were companies such as Med Sun Lines, Intercruise, and the Ulysses Line. Across the seas, for the expanding North American and worldwide cruise markets, there were the likes of Carras Cruises, Royal Cruise Lines, and later Regency Cruises. Alas, many are now gone, victims of changing economics, business miscalculations, disasters or, more recently, buy-outs and mergers.

In retrospect it seems that I have actually sailed on a good number of the ships mentioned in these pages: the *Regal Empress* (ex-*Olympia*), *Carnivale* (ex-*Queen Anna Maria*); and a long string of Chandris ships: *Queen Frederica,*

Ellinis, Britanis, Regina Magna, Romanza, Amerikanis, The Victoria, Carina, Meridien, Horizon, Zenith, Mercury, Galaxy, Infinity, Millennium and *Constellation.* Then there were trips onboard the *Stella Solaris, Stella Maris II, Regent Sun, Jupiter, Olympic Countess, Triton, Atlantis* and possibly even others. The trips were important not only for their ports of call – that exposure to fascinating, far-away places – but also for meeting and often interviewing captains, chief engineers, pursers and hotel directors. There were many stories, tales and notes jotted down, some appearing herein.

I was aboard the Chandris *Horizon* on her maiden voyage from New York to Bermuda in May 1990. She was then the first large new build for Greek owners. Within a company well known for renewing and rebuilding veteran tonnage, she was a reason for great excitement and pride. She was a grand successor to the likes of the earlier *Ellinis, Australis, Romantica* and *Fiesta.*

Another high point was, following an interview with Georges Potomianos, seeing the entire harbor of Piraeus from the rooftop deck of the Epirotiki offices. Passenger ships seemed to be everywhere, in every direction. I had had earlier interviews, also in Piraeus, with Chandris, Med Sun and Festival Cruises. Often, we discussed ships as we watched ships!

Finally, another exciting time was to spend a day or two in the glorious English countryside home and office of Arthur Crook, who, as a Lloyd's surveyor and engineer, had some connection with Greek passenger ships, their refits and repairs, and of course with their owners. He knew many Greek passenger ships, their owners and operators quite intimately. Alone, he is a wealth of insightful, interesting recollections. He also called upon several friends, all of them from the marine architectural and passenger ship design fields, and around a large table, we talked of nothing but ships – passenger ships, of course. My notes filled page after page.

I do not lay claim to mentioning all, or even nearly all, the Greek passenger ships of the past fifty years. Quite simply, there are far too many. This book is more of an overview. Hopefully, however, most of the better known ships and their owners are included. It is, at any rate, a great collection – those wonderful, ever-fascinating *Greek Passenger Ships.*

Bill Miller
Secaucus, New Jersey, USA
December 2005

CHAPTER I

AMBASSADOR CRUISES

As built for the Zim Lines, the West German-constructed *Theodor Herzl* and her sister, the *Jerusalem*, were attractive ships with modern interiors and fully air-conditioned quarters. In addition to their regular sailings within the Mediterranean, mostly between Marseilles or Venice and Haifa, they also made occasional South American sailings, as well as cruises from New York and other US ports. In 1964, Zim planned to convert both ships into all first class cruise ships, but this never came to pass. The *Theodor Herzl* was sold in 1969 to American travel interests and was set to become the *Carnivale*, the

forerunner of Carnival Cruise Lines, but this never came to pass. Instead, she was purchased in 1975 by the Bahama Star Line and renamed *Vera Cruz*. Used in the North American cruise service, she was sold to Ambassador Cruises in 1990 and was to sail as *The Fiesta*, in both Mediterranean and winter Caribbean services. However, while undergoing her conversion, she caught fire at Perama, Greece on October 24th 1991 and was a complete loss. The fire-damaged *The Fiesta* was later salvaged and her remains brought ashore for scrapping.

Opposite left: The trim-looking *Vera Cruz I.* (*Luis Miguel Correia Collection*)

Opposite right: The remains of the fire-damaged ship being salvaged in 1992. (*Antonio Scrimali*)

CHAPTER II

CARRAS CRUISES

THE REBUILT DAPHNE AND DANAE

In the mid-1970s, Greek shipping and real estate tycoon John G. Carras decided to enter the expanding international cruise business. But instead of concentrating on the rather predictable Aegean trades or the mass-market US–Caribbean service, he set about creating two of the world's most luxurious passenger ships. He named them *Daphne* and *Danae*. After extensive redesign and rebuilding work, they entered service in 1975–1976. Their cruises were on roving, international itineraries for the specially created Carras Cruises. But, although they were splendid ships in all ways, the entire project was rather short lived. Sales were low and losses high. Within three years, by 1979, Carras Cruises was dissolved and the two ships placed on long-term charter and later sold outright to Italy's Costa Cruises.

'They were very fine ships with an exceptional sense of spaciousness about them,' remembered John Sherwood, a California-based travel agent who specialized in selling long, luxurious cruises. 'Extra-width corridors, for example, created a great sense of flow between the public rooms,' he added. Public areas included the Muses Main Lounge, a disco, verandah, a cocktail lounge, library and the Symposium Dining Room. Other amenities included an outdoor pool and adjacent splash pool, closed circuit television, a sauna, an algarium (for healthy treatments with the likes of seaweed), a theater,

children's playroom, gift shop, beauty salon, barber shop and onboard marine equipment that included the likes of sailboats and launches.

'Carras had some fascinating itineraries: Europe, South America, the Amazon, around the world. They had the first Western cruise to call in China [1977],' noted Sherwood. 'There was even a trip planned to sail 125 miles along the Hudson River, from New York City to Albany. It would have stopped at West Point as well. It would have been quite unique for such a large cruise ship. But Carras lost out in the end. They were largely unknown to the general traveling public and especially to segments of the important, upper-end of the cruise market. They also faced serious competition, especially from the super deluxe Royal Viking Line. And so the Greek owners lost interest as the bills mounted and mounted.'

The 533-foot-long ships had actually been freighters, built in Britain in the mid-1950s. Owned by the Port Line, a subsidiary of Cunard, the *Daphne* was constructed by Swan, Hunter & Wigham Richardson at Wallsend-on-Tyne as the *Port Sydney*. The *Danae* came from Harland & Wolff at Belfast and had been the *Port Melbourne*. Carrying a dozen passengers as well, they sailed in the so-called 'meat trades', trading between UK ports, Australia and New Zealand. They sailed outwards with general freight and returned with reefer goods. When the Greeks bought them in 1972, the plan was actually to remake them as Mediterranean car ferries, the *Akrotiri Express* and *Therisos Express* respectively. But then plans changed and they were thoroughly rebuilt as 400-passenger cruise ships.

The handsome *Daphne* was a fine example of a conversion of a freighter to luxury cruise ship. *(Michael D. J. Lennon)*

Costa bought the pair outright in 1985. The *Daphne* was later transferred to a Costa-Russian cooperative called Prestige Cruises until sold in 1996. She then became the *Switzerland*, sailing for Swiss owners – Leisure Cruise Lines – again on worldwide cruises. She was then sold to Greek interests, Chios Shipping Company, but at first for German charter cruising. Renamed *Ocean Monarch*, she made relief voyages in 2005 for Tsunami victims in Asia. The *Danae* has had a more involved history. Just before she was to embark on a three-month-long voyage around the world in December 1991, she caught fire while undergoing repairs in a Genoa shipyard. At first declared a total loss and about to be scrapped, she was in fact sold by the marine underwriters to Greek buyers, the Liberian-registered Harbor Maritime. Temporarily, she was renamed *Anar* and later *Starlight Express,* with rumors of a possible charter to Regency Cruises. She was then fully repaired and leased to run German cruise charters as the *Baltica,* but by 1995, her owners were in default and the 17-knot ship arrested. In the winter of 1996, she was again sold, this time to the Lisbon-headquartered Arcalia Shipping Company, owned by Georges Potomianos, a cousin of the Potomianos family that owned Epirotiki Lines. She was then renamed *Princess Danae,* fully refurbished and sent on European as well as South American cruises. Indeed, these two former Carras sisters have had interesting lives.

CHAPTER III

CHANDRIS

SAILING ON THE PATRIS

The first major passenger ship in the Chandris Lines' fleet was the 18,400-ton *Patris*. Built at Harland & Wolff's yard at Belfast in 1950 as Union-Castle Line's *Bloemfontein Castle*, the 595-foot-long ship joined the Greeks nine years later. Her capacity was greatly increased from 721 all cabin class passengers to 1,036 (36 in first class, 1,000 in tourist) and later up to 1,400 for her Chandris owners. A popular as well as very profitable ship, she was suited to her trade: unpretentious passenger quarters blended with a four-hold freight capacity. As the *Patris*, she carried immigrants from Europe out to Australia and then, on the homeward trips, carried budget Australian tourists (the 'backpacker set' as one staff member called it), as well as some disgruntled migrants who were unhappy with Australia. She also returned with large quantities of Australian beef in her freezer compartments, which were left over from her Union Castle days.

Generally, the 18½-knot *Patris* sailed from Piraeus and Limassol to Fremantle, Melbourne and Sydney via Port Said and Aden. First under the advertising name of the Europe-Australia Line, the Chandris 'Down Under' service was a huge success. Soon, a string of even larger second-hand liners were added such as the *Ellinis*, the *Australis,* the *Queen Frederica* and the *Britanis*. These other ships did, however, expand the service to Northern Europe, to Bremerhaven, Rotterdam and Southampton. They were 'full-up' on every outbound sailing,

especially after Anthony Chandris secured the prized Australian Government contract to carry the low-fare, so-called 'new settlers'. Gregory Maxwell, an Australian who had moved to England in the late 1960s, decided to return home for a visit in 1972. He sailed aboard the *Patris*.

'By then, following the closure of the Suez Canal, the *Patris* was sailing out of Djibouti in French Somalia on the East African coast. Chandris flew you down to Djibouti on charter flights,' he recalled. 'The ship was absolutely full – Yugoslavians, Italians, Greeks, Turks, even Arabs. I was the only Anglo-Saxon among the passengers. Djibouti, as I remember, was like Fort de France on Martinique – shops, souvenir stands, a tropical outpost of French imports. We sailed with nearly 1,000 passengers and then picked-up 400 French-speaking passengers at Mauritius. Otherwise, I think that the breakdown was something like 300 Greeks, 200 Italians, 200 Yugoslavians and about 300 Arabs and Turks. What a compliment! There were five different typewriters for the five different languages to make daily programs. The Turkish and Arab migrants were from villages in the mountains or from the desert. They were very primitive, almost barbaric. Everyone else seemed to stay clear of them. I ate in a separate dining room with the Italians. There were three sittings for dinner: 4, 6 and 7.30p.m.'

'Every night during the voyage, everyone was given one free drink,' recalled Maxwell. 'It was watered-down, but a great marketing touch just the same. Chandris was very, very clever. If and when these migrants traveled by ship again, they would think of that drink and remember Chandris Lines. And

they did! The Australian immigration officers came aboard two days before arrival in Melbourne and began the massive processing. It was actually an extraordinary effort. The officials forced these immigrant-passengers to throw out all their canned olives and cheeses and oils and salamis because of quarantine. They all resisted. They cried. They feared that they would starve. The Australian authorities assisted with jobs for these people. But at first, at Melbourne, many of them stayed at the Bonagilla Camp until proper housing could be arranged.'

Soon, however, with rising fuel prices and increased competition from jets that were now regularly flying east of Suez, Chandris had to make further changes. With the likes of the *Ellinis* and the *Britanis* being shifted to almost full-time cruising, the *Patris*, along with the *Australis*, continued the long, but declining Australian run. While the larger ship remained in European service, the *Patris* was soon placed on a far shorter route, from Singapore to Fremantle, Melbourne and Sydney. Now, her passengers were flown out on cheap charter flights to Singapore and then made the final ten or so days by sea.

In 1975, between February and November, the *Patris* was called to a noble task: serving as a temporary accommodation ship for the residents of the Australian city of Darwin, which had been devastated by a tropical storm. In 1976, she returned to the Mediterranean after a long absence for a new, albeit short-lived, Chandris venture: ferry service across the Adriatic between Ancona, Patras and Piraeus. She was specially refitted as well – restyled for 1,000 passengers, with garages for up to 300 cars. This was not a Chandris-type service however, and so in 1979 she was sold to another Greek company, the Karageorgis Lines, and was renamed *Mediterranean Island*. In 1981, she was again renamed, this time becoming *Mediterranean Star*. Her last voyage came in the summer of 1987 when she left Piraeus under tow for the scrap yards in Pakistan as the *Terra*.

Above left: The 8,400-ton *Charlton Star*, ex-*Elisabethville* of the Compagnie Maritime Belge and built in 1921, was the very first Chandris passenger ship. She joined them in 1947, having served with the British during the War as the *Empire Bure*. The 700-passenger *Star* sailed on mostly immigrant and refugee voyages and, in 1958, became the *Maristrella*, also for Chandris. She was scrapped two years later, however, at Osaka, Japan. *(Richard Faber Collection)*

Above right: The first Chandris liner, the *Patris*, was very popular with Greeks on the Australian run *(Frank Andrews)*

Below: The French liner *Bretagne*, seen here at New York's Pier 88 in June 1961, was part of Chandris by 1960 and later became the *Brittany*. *(Author's Collection)*

Top left: The 3,659-ton *Fiesta* was rebuilt from the Isle of Man steamer *Mona's Queen*, built in 1946 and converted by Chandris in 1962–63. *(Chandris Cruises)*

Top right: Also modernized, the *Carina* had been Canadian Pacific's *Princess Helene*, originally completed in 1930. She is seen here arriving in Venice in July 1971. *(Author's Collection)*

Middle left: For their Greek islands and Eastern Mediterranean cruise trades, Chandris Cruises used the *Romantica*, built in 1936 as Furness Withy's *Fort Townshend*. *(V. H. Young & L. A. Sawyer Collection)*

Middle right: The US-flag *Panama,* built in 1939 and used in the New York–Caribbean service, is seen here in the Hudson River in 1947. She joined Chandris in 1965 and became the *Regina*, the flagship of their Chandris Cruises' fleet.

Below left: Similarly, the 4,595-ton *Fantasia* had been restyled after serving as the 1935-built *Duke of York* of British Railways. *(Alex Duncan)*

Below right: The restyled *Regina* and later *Regina Prima* sailed in the Eastern Mediterranean as well as winter Caribbean services. *(Michael D. J. Lennon)*

THE FLAGSHIP AUSTRALIS

For nearly fifteen years, she had been sitting at her Greek moorings not far from Piraeus. Lonely, largely forgotten and certainly falling into deepening decay, the onetime flagship of the entire US merchant marine and later flagship of the Greek merchant fleet, the last-named *American Star* had a long and diverse career. She had survived for an amazing fifty-four years, sailing as a wartime troopship, transatlantic luxury liner, Australian migrant ship and, finally, as a cruise ship. But in January 1994, while under tow and on her way to becoming an ocean liner-style hotel in far-off Thailand, the aged, creaking, almost empty 33,500-ton former luxury ship met her end. In ferocious hurricane winds, her tow lines snapped and she drifted ashore on the north end of the Canary Islands. Then, like a dead, beached whale, old age finally kicked in – her 723-foot-long hull broke into two large pieces.

She is perhaps best remembered as the *America*, built at the Newport News shipyard in Virginia just before the Second World War, in 1937–40. At first diverted to the safety of trans-Panama Canal cruising, she was soon handed over to the Government and, painted in gray and with her capacity enlarged from 1,000 passengers to nearly 9,000 soldiers, she sailed for the next four years as the USS *West Point*. She traveled almost everywhere – Europe, the South Pacific, the Indian Ocean, South America. Often a target to enemy bombers and subs, she was decommissioned intact in 1946 and then rehabilitated for Atlantic luxury service between New York, Southampton, Le Havre and Bremerhaven. Then a three-class ship, she was America's finest and largest liner until the first arrival, in June 1952, of the super liner *United States*, the fastest passenger ship ever built. The 23-knot *America* became her consort.

Then still using the Greek flag, Chandris Lines bought her in October 1964 for their Europe–Australia migrant trade and around-the-world tourist run. Rebuilt as the gray-hulled *Australis*, her capacity was more than doubled, jumping from 1,046 to as many as 2,258, all in tourist class. She was the largest Greek-owned passenger ship yet and sailed with Chandris until November 1977. According to Arthur Crook, 'Greek ship-owners preferred American passenger ships first and British ones second. They went for good prices and especially because American ships were spacious and therefore ideal to rebuild. Ships such as the *Australis* were also the early training for thousands of Greek officers and seamen. Chandris itself was said to be the greatest training ground in the entire Greek merchant marine. Later, Festival Cruises was half ex-Chandris. Crew members also felt that Chandris, in the 1960s and 1970s, was among the top three Greek companies for employment and as a future recommendation. Sun Line was said to be at the top, Epirotiki was second and Chandris was third. Everyone else was fourth.'

The following year, in May 1978, she was back in New York, as the renamed *America,* but ran no more than two highly unsuccessful short cruises. Her owners, the Venture Cruise Lines, were forced into bankruptcy by claims of poor food, backed-up toilets and even garbage in the swimming pools. Chandris bought back their old flagship and, as the *Italis* and minus her forward 'dummy' stack, placed her in Mediterranean cruising. But by late 1979, she was too old and too expensive, and so was sent off to an anchorage in Perama Bay, a great basin of idle ships of all kinds and sizes. She passed to new owners and became the *Alferdoss* and then the *Noga* and finally the *American Star*. Over the years, there were rumors of all sorts: a floating hotel in West Africa, a prison ship in Texas, a marina in Montreal, a convention center annex in New York, a casino in Australia. Once sold, in 1993, for the Thai hotel project, she did undergo some repairs in preparation for the long, slow tow out to the East. Her departure was long delayed and then, because the Suez Canal authorities refused permission for her passage, a big tug guided her out of the Mediterranean and through the Straits of Gibraltar for the trip around Africa and then across the Indian Ocean. Four crewmen, who were aboard the otherwise empty, almost darkened ship, were rescued by helicopter off the Canaries after the tow lines snapped.

The aft piece of the wreckage later broke free and slipped into the Atlantic. By 2001, there were reports that the 400-feet of the forward section might be blasted free by the Spanish navy since it had become dangerous and troublesome. The aft section eventually fell into the sea, and the forward section was reportedly collapsing in late 2005.

THE BELOVED BRITANIS

In October 1931, when the liner *Monterey* was launched at Quincy, Massachusetts, the managers and the directors, the designers and the building crews could never have imagined that their creation would reach her sixty-eighth year. What a solid ship! And what history! And especially, what a tribute to American design and construction of that time! The *Monterey* later became the Chandris *Britanis* and, in 1994, was still making twice-weekly cruises out of Miami as well as an annual seven-week trip around continental South America. She was then the world's second oldest deep-sea cruise ship. Only Epirotiki's little *Argonaut* of 1929 had a few years on her. Her amazing record was also a tribute to Chandris, who sailed her in the end and so lovingly maintained her.

'She is in very good condition. Very strong and very solid,' said one of her last masters, Captain George Panagiotakis, in July 1992 when the ship turned sixty. 'We are still using the original steam turbines. Of course, these require constant maintenance. We repair and replace parts immediately. Even though most of the manufacturers are out of business, we do not have much of a problem with spares. We even have them custom-made, if necessary, in the United States, in the UK and in Greece. Some other parts came from the near-sister *Ellinis* [scrapped in 1987], but which had been the original Matson *Lurline* of 1932. In fact, she had parts from the *Homeric* [scrapped 1974], which was the *Mariposa* of 1931. There were also parts from the *Queen Frederica* [scrapped 1978], the former *Malolo* of 1927. So you might say that all the big Matson liners live-on in the *Britanis*.'

Captain Panagiotakis had first joined the *Britanis* in 1971, on the old Chandris liner service out to Australia. 'It took four weeks to sail from Southampton to Sydney via South Africa,' he recalled. 'We were usually routed via Lisbon, Las Palmas or Tenerife, Cape Town, then Fremantle, Melbourne and Sydney. From there, we would sometimes make a cruise with all-Australian passengers and to places like Suva, Lautoka, Apia and Papeete. These would be two-week voyages usually. Afterward, we would resume the "line voyage" via Wellington, Tahiti, Acapulco, the Panama Canal, Curacao or San Juan, Port Everglades and finally home to Southampton. The full voyage would take about seventy-five days. Outbound, we would sail completely full – 1,600 migrants bound for Australia. Homewards, we would be about 75 per cent full, about 1,200 passengers in all, and this was mostly budgeted tourists and backpackers and large families on holiday.'

The 638-foot-long *Britanis* was built by Bethlehem Steel and was commissioned in April 1932 for the Matson Line's South Pacific route: San Francisco and Los Angeles to the Pacific islands, New Zealand and Australia. As the first *Monterey*, she was teamed with the original *Mariposa*. The *Lurline* and the *Malolo* looked after the Hawaiian run. The war disrupted these services and then, with a heroic record of long passages, hundreds of thousands of troops and even a major rescue to her credit, the *Monterey* was returned to Matson. But she was sent almost directly to 'mothballs'. It seemed that restoration costs were unaffordable, at least until the mid-1950s when she was modernized and upgraded as the 'new' *Matsonia*. She had her debut in May 1957, and was placed on the Honolulu service alongside the *Lurline*. In 1963, however, when her running-mate was withdrawn and sold (to Chandris, in fact, to become the *Ellinis*), the *Matsonia* took on that more

popular Matson name. She became Matson's last Hawaiian liner, sailing on until sold to Chandris herself in 1970.

The *Britanis* began cruising full-time in 1975 (at first divided between European and Caribbean waters) and in permanent US service since 1981. She did mostly short cruises and, to start with, mostly out of New York. She sailed up to Halifax, Martha's Vineyard, Boston, New London and even attended the America's Cup Races at Newport. There were also luncheon cruises from 9.30 in the morning until 2.30 in the afternoon. By 1992, she was the only ship making two-day cruises out of Miami to Nassau. These were 'party cruises' that were popular for dancing and gambling.

Brad Hatry, a former chairman of the World Ship Society's Port of New York Branch, did nine cruises on the *Britanis*. 'She was a favorite, a great ship and so very affordable,' he recalled. 'I sailed on her from New York as well as Miami. She was a ship buff's ship. She had great history in that sixty-year-long career. You can almost feel the past onboard her. She was sturdy, well run, offered good Chandris cuisine and offered great value.'

At sixty, in the summer of 1992, the *Britanis* seemed to glow. She was snow white from stem to stern, capped by a pair of distinctive blue and black stacks bearing white Xs (the X is the Greek initial for 'Ch' in the Chandris name). Reports from the Chandris engineering department were then that she could last another ten years. How proud! How wonderful! 'Dimitri Kaparis, the vice president of Chandris operations, personally looked after the *Britanis* by constantly making repairs, especially to her pipes,' noted Arthur Crook. 'He kept adding what he called "Band-Aids".'

Alas, she was finally withdrawn from cruise service in 1994. She did a stint under charter to the US Government as a refugee accommodation ship in Guantanamo Bay in Cuba, but then was laid up in the backwaters of Tampa, Florida. Her neighbors at various times included the likes of the *Regent Sea*, the *Regent Sun* and the *Regent Rainbow*. By 1999, reports were that the *Britanis*, by then sold to intermediary buyers and renamed *Belophin I*, would be refitted as an Art Deco-style 'boutique hotel' and moored along the San Francisco waterfront were promising. Her stacks might even have been repainted in Matson Line colors and her name changed to *Normandie*, a reminder of the great French liner of the 1930s. But as always, problems, mostly financial ones, for such floating hotel projects killed all plans. In July 2000, she left Tampa under tow, bound for a long, slow voyage around South Africa to the scrap yards at Alang in India. She took on water off Brazil, but managed to continue. Under windy conditions, she began to capsize near Cape Town and later sank.

Above left: When the *America* resumed transatlantic service for the United States Lines in November 1946, she was the largest, fastest and finest passenger ship in the US merchant marine. *(Cronican-Arroyo Collection)*

Above right: The *America* had superb interiors, as seen in this view of the two-deck high first class main lounge, and many of these were retained by the Chandris Lines when the ship became the *Australis* in 1965. *(Cronican-Arroyo Collection)*

Below left: The same ship's superb Smoking Room. *(Cronican-Arroyo Collection)*

Below right: Anchored during a cruise visit, the *Australis* was, for some years, the largest liner in the Greek fleet. *(Michael D. J. Lennon)*

Clockwise from top left:

The *Australis* was revived for a short time in 1978 as the cruise ship *America*. *(Author's Collection)*

Abandoned and broken in two, the *American Star* has come to the end of her days. *(Steven L. Tacey Collection)*

One of the most popular ships in the Greek passenger fleet, the 21,500-ton *Queen Frederica* joined Chandris Lines in 1965. *(Author's Collection)*

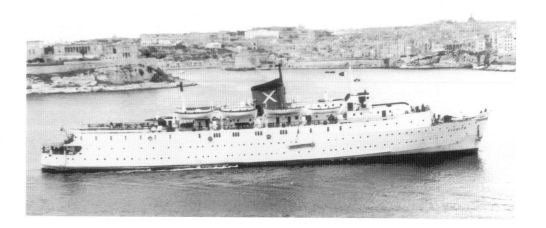

Clockwise from top left:
The distinctive Chandris funnel markings as seen aboard the *Amerikanis*. *(Author's Collection)*

The 1952-built *Kenya Castle* used in Union Castle Line's London-Around-Africa service, joined Chandris in 1967. *(Alex Duncan)*

Thoroughly rebuilt and modernized, the *Kenya Castle* began sailing as the *Amerikanis* in August 1968. *(Author's Collection)*

Another converted ferry, British Rail's *Amsterdam* became the *Fiorita* for Chandris Cruises in 1970. *(Antonio Scrimali)*

Clockwise from top left:
Built in 1944, the American troopship *General W.P. Richardson* went into passenger service in 1949 and therein began a long succession of names: *Laguardia, Leilani, President Roosevelt, Atlantis* (for Chandris), *Emerald Seas* (seen here at Miami), *Fantastica, Funtastica, Terrifica, Sun Fiesta* and finally *Ocean Explorer I* for Greeks known as Excellence Holdings. After a long career, she was scrapped in India in 2004. *(Luis Miguel Correia)*

The immensely successful and much beloved *Britanis* had been Matson Line's *Monterey* of 1932 and then later sailed as the *Matsonia* and *Lurline*. She survived for some sixty-eight years, until she sank off South Africa in July 2000 on her way, under tow, to Indian ship breakers. *(Luis Miguel Correia)*

The *Regina Magna* had been built in 1939 as the French *Pasteur* and then sailed, from 1959 until 1971, as the *Bremen* for North German Lloyd. Retired by Chandris Cruises in 1974, she later became a mid-Eastern accommodation ship before sinking in the Indian Ocean while on route to scrappers on Taiwan in June 1980. *(Author's Collection)*

The 6,600-ton *Ariane* was another of the smaller Chandris cruise ships. She had been Swedish Lloyd's *Patricia*, built in 1951, and later Hamburg America Line's *Ariadne*. Chandris bought her in 1972, but she quickly began a charter as the *Freeport II* and then as *Bon Vivant* and, in 1978, as *Ariane*. She was sold to Cypriot buyers in 1989 and renamed *Empress Katerina* before being scrapped in 1997. *(Michael D. J. Lennon)*

The *Romanza* dated originally from 1939, having been the *Huascran* of Hamburg America Line, then Canadian Pacific's *Beaverbrae* and, from 1955 until 1970, the Italian *Aurelia*. In 1990, she joined Ambassador Cruises and became their *Romantica*. She caught fire in the eastern Mediterranean in October 1997 and her charred remains were scrapped a year later. *(Antonio Scrimali)*

Above left: Perama Bay in Greece was a vast holding area for both out-of-work and retired ships. The *Regina Magna* is at the far end of this view, dated April 1977.

Above right: The *Victoria* had been Union Castle's *Dunnottar Castle* of 1936, but was rebuilt in 1958–1959 for the Incres Line. She joined Chandris in 1976. *(Michael D. J. Lennon)*

Right: The *Meridian* was rebuilt in 1990 for the Celebrity Cruises, the more up-scale division of Chandris that was created especially for a series of newbuilds. The former *Galileo Galilei*, she is seen here at New York. *(Author's Collection)*

Below: The *Azur*, a former car ferry, joined Chandris in 1987 and is seen here at St Thomas in January 1988. *(Author's Collection)*

Above: The *Horizon*, shown arriving in New York harbor on her maiden voyage in May 1990, was the first newly built passenger ship in the Chandris fleet. She was assigned to their Celebrity Cruises division. *(Author's Collection)*

Above right: Following the great success of the 47,000-ton *Horizon* and her sister, the *Zenith*, added in 1992, Celebrity built three new 77,000-ton sisterships – the 76,000-ton *Century, Galaxy* (shown here being fitted out at Meyerwerft at Papenburg) and *Mercury*, added in 1995–1997. *(Jurgen Saupe)*

Right: The success of the Century Class led to four 91,000-ton sisters: *Millennium* (shown outbound at Valletta, Malta), *Infinity, Summit* and *Constellation*. These ships were commissoned in 2000–2002. Next, for 2008, Celebrity is adding the 113,000-ton Challenger Class. *(Michael Cassar)*

CHAPTER IV

DOLPHIN CRUISE LINES

Above left: Dolphin Cruise Lines ran Miami–Bahamas cruises, using the 8,987-ton, 588-passenger *Dolphin VI*. The Zim Lines combination passenger–cargo liner *Zion*, shown docking at New York's Pier 64 in 1961, became Portugal's *Amelia De Mello* in 1966 and then was rebuilt as the Greek cruise ship *Ithaca* in 1972. In 1979, she became the *Dolphin VI*. *(Richard K. Morse Collection)*

Above right: Seen here at Miami, the *Dolphin VI* sailed until 2001 and then was broken-up in India. *(Luis Miguel Correia)*

CHAPTER V

DOLPHIN-HELLAS SHIPPING COMPANY

Above left: The Furness-Bermuda liner *Ocean Monarch*, a 13,600-tonner, completed in 1951, was a favorite cruise ship, especially popular on the New York–Bermuda run. She was sold in 1966, however, becoming Bulgaria's *Varna*. Laid-up in 1973–74, she was sold to Greek buyers in 1978, supposedly to be revived as the *Riviera* for Mediterranean cruising. This soon changed to a plan to rename her *Venus* for New York–Bermuda service. But in 1980–81, her owners were finally became Dolphin-Hellas Shipping Company for European cruising and she was named the *Reina Del Mar*. But while being refitted at Perama, on May 28th 1981, she was destroyed by fire and then capsized. She was a total loss. *(Antonio Scrimali)*

Above right: Dolphin-Hellas bought the former Bergen Line's 6,600-ton *Leda*, long popular on the Newcastle–Bergen run, in 1981. She had last served as an accommodation ship for North Sea oil rig crews. Renamed *Albatross*, she did some charter cruising before, in 1988–89, she was to be the *Betsy Ross* for the short-lived, Greek-owned American Star Line.

Clockwise from top right:

Dolphin-Hellas also bought the laid-up *Rasa Sayang*, a Far Eastern cruise ship that had been Norwegian America Line's *Bergensfjord*, an 18,739-tonner built in 1956 for transatlantic service between Oslo and New York as well as considerable cruising. She became the French Line's *De Grasse* in 1971 and then was sold to other Norwegian buyers two years later for cruising out of Singapore. But after a fire in 1977, she was laid-up and later sold to Dolphin-Hellas, who renamed her *Golden Moon* and then arranged for a Dutch charter as the *Prins Van Oranje*. When this failed to materialize, the plan was to lease her to London-based CTC Lines for Australian cruising, again as the *Rasa Sayang*. But while being refitted at Perama, on August 27th 1980, she caught fire and later sank. Her remains were left quite close to another ill-fated Dolphin-Hellas ship, the *Reina Del Mar*, which burned and then sank nine months later. The 577-foot-long *Rasa Sayang* is seen here at Valletta, Malta. *(Steffen Weirauch Collection)*

Another member of the Dolphin-Hellas fleet is the former Zim Lines ro-ro ship *Narcis*, which became the Greek *Alkyon* in 1985 and then the *Aegean Dolphin* a year later. She was converted to a 576-passenger cruise ship in 1988 and later sailed for Renaissance Cruises and then Golden Sun Cruises. The 461-foot-long vessel was originally built in Rumania and is seen here at Valletta in August 1997. *(Michael Cassar)*

The *Betsy Ross* later became the *Amalfi*, sailing under charter to Starlauro Cruises. But again, unsuccessful and in debt, she was laid-up at Venice and later scrapped at Aliaga in Turkey *(Selim San)*

CHAPTER VI

EFTHYMIADIS LINES

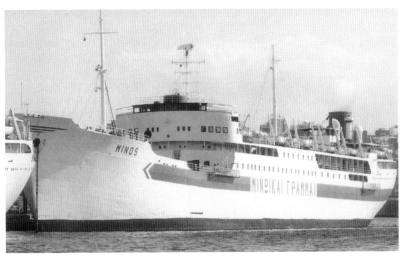

Above left: Greek ship owner Constantine S. Efthymiadis decided to enter the passenger ship business in the early 1960s, but in a unique way – by converting oil tankers into passenger ships. He saw this as an agreeable alternative, at least in the beginning, to either building new tonnage or acquiring and converting second-hand passenger ships. His first conversion was the 496-foot-long Swedish tanker *Maria Gorthon*, which, in 1963, was made over to carry 670 cabin and deck passengers as well as up to 200 cars and small trucks in 'drive-on, drive-off' garages cut along the ship's sides. The 8,785-ton ship, originally built in 1951, was renamed *Phaistos* and began sailing between Piraeus and Crete. Laid-up in 1977, she was subsequently scrapped. *(Michael Cassar)*

Above right: The 10,731-ton *Minos* followed in 1965. Built at Malmo, Sweden in 1952, she had been the tanker *Soya-Margareta*. Diesel-driven and with a single screw, she was like her converted fleetmates in being capable of top speeds of only 14 knots. The 533-foot-long ship also sailed between Piraeus and Crete. She was withdrawn in 1977, following the complete collapse of Efthymiadis Lines, as it was called, and later sailed for other Greek owners, Lesvos Maritime Company, before being scrapped. *(Michael Cassar)*

Above left: The *Sophia* was the third conversion, having been the Swedish tanker *Soya-Birgitta*. At 9,000 tons, she had been built in 1953 and then rebuilt in 1966 for some 670 passengers and 200 autos. She sank, however, in 1976. *(Antonio Scrimali)*

Above right: The fourth and last of these tanker conversions was the 11,232-ton *Heleana*, built as the *Munkedal* in 1954 and then rebuilt in 1966. She was used on the Adriatic, sailing between Ancona and Patras, but then later, in 1977, sank in the same waters. Subsequent inquiries proved that she was improperly and therefore unsafely loaded and this prompted the Greek Government to close down Efthymiadis, by then the owners of over a dozen passenger ships, and seize their fleet. The owners themselves were sent to prison for negligence. *(Michael Cassar)*

Below left: Efthymiadis bought several other passenger ships in the mid-1960s and also decided to expand into the blossoming Mediterranean cruise trade. The 9,931-ton *Lindos*, for example, was acquired in 1967, after having been the 1952-built *Lyuatey* for France's Compagnie de Navigation Paquet. She traded mostly on the Marseilles-West Africa route until the 1960s when she briefly sailed to the Eastern Mediterranean as the *Galilee*. As the *Lindos*, the 465-footer sailed mostly between Piraeus and Limassol via Rhodes until retired and then scrapped in 1975. *(Alex Duncan)*

Below right: The first noted venture by Efthymiadis into cruising were the thorough conversions of two French passenger-cargo ships, the sisters *Azrou* and *Azemmour*, formerly of Compagnie de Navigation Paquet and used on the Marseilles–Casablanca run. The 1949-built, 3,900-ton *Azrou* was sold to Efthymiadis in 1968 and became the totally rebuilt *Melina*; the *Azemmour*, also 1951, went to these Greek owners a year later and was reconstructed as the *Delos*. Both ships were given rather high standard accommodations for up to 500 one-class passengers. All cabins, for example, had private facilities and the public areas included a showroom, disco and outdoor pool. Generally, the two sisters sailed on seven-day cruises from Piraeus to the Greek isles and Turkey. *(Michael Cassar)*

Above left: Beginning in 1968, Efthymiadis continued, but with something of a preference for out-of-work French passenger-cargo liners and quickly bought no less than six additional ships. The Company bought all four, 10,900-ton sisters of Messageries Maritimes' *Ferdinand de Lesseps* class. The *de Lesseps* was rebuilt as the *Delphi* and later sailed as *La Perla* and then *La Palma* before being scrapped in 2003. The *La Bourdonnais* became the *Knossos*, but was disabled by an engine room fire off Cyprus on May 3rd 1973. She was soon scrapped. The *Pierre Loti* became the *Olimpia* and then the *Patra* for Efthymiadis and, in 1978, joined a subsidiary to become the *Chrysovalandou II* and then the *Eros*. She was scrapped in 1986. Finally, the former *Jean La Borde* became the *Mykinai* and then the *Ancona*. She was renamed *Brindisi Express* in 1974 and afterward did a Singapore-based charter as the *Eastern Princess*. She was sold to Epirotiki Lines in 1976 and rebuilt as their *Oceanos*. She sank off South Africa after taking on water and flooding on August 4th 1991. One other ex-French ship, the 12,700-ton *Caledonien*, was acquired in 1972 and became the *Nisos Kypros* and then *Island of Cyprus* before being scrapped in 1975. *(Michael Cassar)*

Above right: End of the line: four Efthymiadis passenger ships are nested together in Eleusis Bay awaiting their fates in 1977. The converted tanker *Phaistos* is on the left, the *Melina* is next, the *Arcadi* (ex-*Président de Cazalet*, also ex-French) and finally the *Delos*. The once popular Efthymiadis fleet was gradually being dispersed. *(Antonio Scrimali)*

Both ships did prove, however, to be mechanically troublesome. They were laid up in 1977 following the collapse of their owners and later offered for sale. The *Melina* went to the breakers in 1980, but not before her engines were removed and placed aboard the *Delos*, which was sold to Aquaviva Shipping Company for Adriatic cruising as the *Bella Maria*. Major engine troubles began on her second voyage and she was later towed to Piraeus and laid-up. To this day, the 373-foot-long ship remains abandoned just outside Piraeus harbor, not far from Atalanti Island. (Author's Collection)

CHAPTER VII

EPIROTIKI LINES

His corner office had huge, panoramic windows that overlooked all the ships in the inner harbor of Piraeus. Luxury cruise liners were in port for the day while a seemingly endless parade of ferries, some of them quite large, came and went constantly. In the office itself, a large bookcase was topped by Company commemoratives: photos and paintings and those plaques that mark special occasions or were gifts from tourist authorities, travel groups, airlines. A long, gloss black desk contained neatly stacked folders of paperwork and documentation that goes with operating a large fleet of cruise ships. Three phones sat in one corner and a secretary came and went, barely making a sound. I was sitting across from one of the last Greek passenger ship magnates, George Potomianos, then president and part owner of the Epirotiki Lines. The Company had the largest cruise fleet still under the Greek flag and, in an intended two-ship exchange, Miami-based Carnival Cruise Lines had just obtained a 43 per cent share in Epirotiki. The Greeks were given the former *Carnivale*, but the transfer of the second ship, the ex-*Mardi Gras*, never materialized. The date was August 1993.

The Potomianos family were in shipping for decades, but only started passenger services later, in the 1950s, using secondhand, and often older, but always quite profitable tonnage. The Company is actually credited with starting modern-day cruising to the Greek islands. In 1955, their 1,900-ton, 185-passenger *Semiramis* began sailing on three- and four-day cruises from Piraeus to such ports as Mykonos, Delos, Santorini and Rhodes. She

was such a big success that others such as the Sun Line, Chandris Cruises, Typaldos Lines and the Efthymiadis Lines followed in her wake. The Greek islands cruise business actually began to boom by the mid-1960s. Other Epirotiki passenger ships followed the *Semiramis* and these included the 2,500-ton *Hermes I* and the 1,500-ton *Atreus*.

By the early 1960s the Company's largest passenger ships were a pair of 5,000 tonners that were actually combination cruise vessels, regular passenger ships, as well as car ferries. Named *Hermes* and *Pegasus*, they had been built back in 1930 as the *Princess Joan* and the *Princess Elizabeth* respectively for Canadian Pacific's Northwestern service between Seattle, Victoria and Vancouver. For the Greeks, the pair maintained Epirotiki's so-called 'express line to the mid-east', from Venice to Corfu, Piraeus, Rhodes, Limassol and Haifa. They carried passengers in three classes: 180 in first class, 140 in cabin class and 150 in tourist.

By 1964, then wanting to offer more luxurious cruises, the Company bought the little Florida-based cruise ship *Orion* and had her thoroughly rebuilt for only 200 guests as the *Argonaut*. Once a private yacht, she had been built by Krupps of Germany in 1929. Three years later, in 1967, a virtually brand new ship, the 3,700-ton *Jason*, was added for extended cruise service. Further conversions included the *Orpheus* and the *Apollo XI*. Charter cruising remained a part of the Company's business and, in October 1968, the *Orpheus* was chartered to Britain's Skyway-Ensign Tours for no less than sixty-eight

Epirotiki Brothers, later and better known as Epirotiki Lines, entered passenger service just before the start of the Second World War, in 1939, with the 4,044-ton *Georgios Potamianos*, the former *Glenrazan*. She was followed by the 1898-built *Attiki*, added in 1948 and lost three years later, and then the 1,964-ton *Calabar*, a small passenger ship built in 1935 for Britain's Elder Dempster Lines for the West African coastal run. She was sold to Epirotiki in 1953 and was refitted as the cruise ship *Semiramis*. This 190-passenger ship is said to have been the first Greek-owned Aegean cruise ship, running three- and four-day trips to the nearby islands. She remained in service until 1979 and was later scrapped. *(Luis Miguel Correia Collection)*

seven-day cruises from Lisbon to Casablanca, Tangier, Malaga, Cadiz and the Algarve. It then ranked as the largest charter of a cruise ship on record. Later, the same ship was chartered to Seattle-based West Line for a summer series of seven-day Alaska cruises and, in winter, to the Mexican Riviera. In 1970, the little *Semiramis* ran some experimental cruises from Palma de Majorca.

In the 1970s, Epirotiki's cruise business expanded considerably. The Aegean trade was booming, thanks to healthy influxes of British and American tourists on land tours but also wanting a touch of the Greek islands. There was also the lucrative and expanding charter cruise market that included sailings up to Norway, the Baltic and around the British Isles. In winter, when part of the fleet was customarily laid-up near Piraeus, there were now itineraries to South America, the Caribbean, even along the Amazon and, on the Pacific side, to the Galapagos. A succession of refitted ships were added: the *Jupiter*, the former *Moledet* of the Zim Lines; Holland America's *Ryndam*, which became the Company flagship *Atlas*; Paquet Cruises' splendid *Rennaisance*, which changed her name only slightly, to *World Renaissance*; and then another former French ship, the *Jean La Borde*, which was run as the *Oceanos*. Epirotiki's resourceful engineers even encouraged the purchase of damaged cruise ships: Bergen Line's fire-ravaged *Meteor* became the *Neptune* and the half-sunken *Sundancer* was revived as the *Pegasus*.

But still bigger ships were ahead, especially in the early 1990s. Norwegian Cruise Lines' 14,000-ton *Sunward II*, herself the former *Cunard Adventurer*, became the *Triton* in 1991. Soon afterward, the 20,000-ton *Carla Costa*, the ex-French Line *Flandre*, was re-christened as the *Pallas Athena*. Then, in 1993, in that joint deal with Carnival, their 27,000-ton *Mardi Gras*, formerly the *Empress of Canada* of Canadian Pacific, was to become the next Company flagship, the *Olympic*, with an Aegean debut in March 1994. But the latter swap never materialized and instead she went to run one-night gambling cruises in the Gulf of Mexico as the *Star of Texas*. Epirotiki owned and managed her, however. Another Carnival ship, the *Fiesta Marina*, the onetime *Empress of Britain* and later the *Queen Anna Maria* and then the *Carnivale*, was to become the *Homeric*, but then took the name *Olympic* instead. The intended *Olympic*, ex-*Empress of Canada*, did, however, later join Epirotiki (in 1995), but as the *Apollon*.

Sadly, misfortune has also been a part of Epirotiki's more recent history. In quick succession, four cruise ships were lost. The *Jupiter* sank in 1988 after a collision in Piraeus harbor; the *Pegasus* burned at Venice in June 1991; two months later the *Oceanos* sank off South Africa in stormy seas; and then, in March 1994, the *Pallas Athena* burned at Piraeus. New tonnage, namely the former *Cunard Countess*, was soon added.

In 1995, Epirotiki Lines, needing to be more efficient and competitive, and to cut rising operational costs, merged with a onetime rival, the Sun Line. Together they created Royal Olympic Cruises. However, the combined companies collapsed into bankruptcy in 2004 and finished sailing within the following year.

Above left: Another early Epirotiki passenger ship was the *Atreus*, which had been Denmark's *Aalborghus*, built in 1913. This 1,554-ton, 464-passenger vessel sailed under the Greek flag from 1958 until 1968, and then was scrapped in 1970. *(Epirotiki Lines)*

Above right: The 5,251-ton *Pegasus*, seen here at Valletta with the Rumanian flagship *Transylvania* in the background, joined Epirotiki in 1961 and had an extensive refitting. She had been the three-funnel *Princess Elizabeth*, built in 1930 for Canadian Pacific's Seattle–Victoria–Vancouver service. Under the Greek flag, she carried some 500 passengers in three classes and up to 120 automobiles. She spent her final years as a floating hotel for oil drilling crews in Scotland before being scrapped in Holland in 1976. Her sister, the *Hermes*, the former *Princess Joan*, also finished her days as accommodation ship in Scotland before going to the breakers in 1974. *(Michael Cassar)*

Below left: The 4,007-ton *Argonaut* had been a private luxury yacht until converted for commercial cruising by Epirotiki in 1965. Built in 1929, she later sailed as the *Regina Maris* before being scrapped in 2003. *(Michael D. J. Lennon)*

Below right: The 3,719-ton ferry *Aphrodite*, built by the Italians in 1965 as reparations to the Greeks (along with two sisters that would become the *Atlantis* of K Lines-Hellenic Cruises and the *Stella Oceanis* for Sun Line), was sold to Epirotiki in 1967 for refitting as the 325-passenger *Jason*. *(Luis Miguel Correia Collection)*

Above left: The 4,303-ton *Odysseus* joined Epirotiki in 1966, after having been the *Leinster* and later the *Ulster Prince* for Irish Sea passenger service. First renamed *Adria*, she became the *Odysseus* for various Mediterranean services, carrying up to 450 passengers and sixty autos. Her final years were spent up in Scotland, serving as a workers' accommodation ship, before being scrapped in 1979. *(Michael Cassar)*

Above right: Another ship added to Epirotiki fleet in 1969 was the 4,145-ton *Orpheus*, which had been rebuilt from the 1948-constructed *Munster*, also used on the Irish Sea run. Provisionally renamed *Theseus* by the Greeks, she was later refitted for cruising, carrying 368 one-class passengers. Seen here at Lisbon in June 1991, she often sailed in later years on charter to Britain's Swan Hellenic Cruises. She was broken-up in 2001. *(Luis Miguel Correia)*

Below left: The 3,824-ton *Apollo 11*, also used for cruising, had been the *Irish Coast*, completed in 1952. She had a string of early, but brief names under Epirotiki: *Orpheus*, *Semiramis I* and *Achilleus*. *(Luis Miguel Correia)*

Below right: The 7,811-ton *Jupiter*, seen here docked at Valletta, joined Epirotiki in 1971 and was refitted for cruising, carrying up to 480 passengers. Built at St Nazaire in 1961, she had been the *Moledet* of Zim Lines. Her career ended in October 1998 when, following a collision just outside Piraeus harbor, she sank quickly. *(Michael Cassar)*

THE CONVERTED ATLAS

'I went up to Rotterdam with Tassos Potomianos and did the preliminary planning for the conversion of the *Ryndam*,' noted Arthur Crook. 'She was an impressive ship and in very good condition in ways and so Potomianos wanted her, but she was single screw. There was a rule at the time that there could be no added single-screw passenger ships under the Greek flag. And so, Tassos got himself made Minister of Marine Affairs for a month and changed that rule!'

The 503-foot-long *Ryndam* and her sister *Maasdam* (later the *Stefan Batory*) had been important transatlantic passenger ships: they introduced high-standard, tourist class dominance. First class had less than ten per cent of the ships' accommodation and was relegated to the small, top-deck area. Tourist, with rates beginning at $20 a day, had the far larger areas and greater facilities, including an outdoor pool and movie theater. Soon, other Atlantic liners were copying their pattern, eliminating the traditional three-class pattern and concentrating on the growing tourist class market. The two ships sailed between Rotterdam, Le Havre, Southampton and New York, and in later years to Quebec City and Montreal. They also ran occasional cruises. In 1967–68, the 16-knot *Ryndam* made mostly student crossings and cruises and for a time was renamed *Waterman*. She was laid-up, however, by 1971 as Holland America Line was preparing to reorganize as Holland America Cruises and concentrate on the leisure market, mostly in the United States.

'Once in Greek service, the *Atlas*,' recalled by Crook, 'was always short of electric power and so Andreas Potomianos used to buy second hand generators and placed them all over the ship. In the end, there were twelve of them onboard.'

'The exterior of the *Atlas* was designed by a young designer named John Bannerman,' he added. 'Epirotiki wanted something new and different and sleek that would match or surpass the new Karageorgis ferries, the sleek *Mediterranean Sea* and *Mediterranean Sky*. Karageorgis was threatening then and Greek shipowners were extremely competitive. There was also the appearance of the greatly rebuilt *Stella Solaris* for another rival company, the Sun Line. They were, of course, all older, rebuilt ships, but they had to look new, modern, stylish.'

The great slowdown in the Mediterranean in 1985–1986 finished off the *Atlas*. She was often laid up, canceled sailings and made at least one cruise with as few as fifty passengers aboard. Other ships and their owners were suffering as well. She was soon sold off, becoming the gambling ship *Pride of Mississippi* and later the *Pride of Galveston* for short gambling jaunts in the Gulf of Mexico out of US ports. She was decommissioned from actual sailings by 1993, but then found further life a year later at Gulfport, Mississippi as the permanently moored casino ship *Copa Casino*.

Above: Bergen Line's little cruiseship *Meteor*, built in 1954 and seriously damaged by a fire in May 1971 while sailing near Vancouver, was declared a total loss until reprieved and sold to Epirotiki for repairs and refitting in Greece. She became the *Neptune*, seen here at Valletta with the *Stella Oceanis* nearby. Laid-up in later years, she was finally scrapped in India in 2001. *(Michael Cassar)*

Below: Holland America's 15,015-ton *Ryndam*, built in 1951 and used on the transatlantic run, was purchased by Epirotiki in August 1972 and had a $2.5 million refit and modernization during which she became the *Atlas*. This 731-berth ship was Epirotiki's chief competition to Sun Line's then new flagship, the *Stella Solaris*. Sold in 1986 to American interests, she ran short-distance gambling cruises in Gulf of Mexico waters, first as the *Pride of Mississippi* and then as the *Pride of Galveston*. Worn out by 1993, she was sold to Nevada gambling interests who used her as the permanently moored *Copa Casino* at Gulfport, Mississippi. She sank in the Caribbean, in March 2004, while being towed and on the way to Indian breakers. *(Michael D. J. Lennon)*

Above: In 1976, Epirotiki took the former French combination passenger-cargo ship *Jean La Borde*, originally built in 1952, and rebuilt her as the cruise ship *Oceanos*. Previously, with Efthymiadis Lines since 1970, she had been the *Mykinai, Brindisi Express* and *Eastern Princess*. Rebuilt with 800 berths, she often cruised under charter, including a stint to Italy's Lauro Line. She had a sad ending, however, when, on August 4th 1991, during a charter cruise in South African waters, she began to leak and then flood. With her engines disabled, she finally sank in rough seas. *(Michael Cassar)*

Below: The Spanish-built *Princesa Isabel*, completed in 1962 for Brazilian owners, was sold in 1969 to Australia's Dominion Far East Line, who sailed her as the *Marco Polo*. Later sold to K Lines-Hellenic Cruises, she was renamed *Aquamarine* and used on some of the earliest tourist cruises to Communist China. Epirotiki bought her in 1988 and refitted her as the 363-passenger *Odysseus*. She was sold out of the bankrupt Royal Olympia fleet in 2005, joining Island Cruises, becoming the *Joy Wave*. *(Michael Cassar)*

Above: The 11,429-ton *World Renaissance* had been the *Renaissance*, built in 1966 for France's Paquet Lines. She joined Epirotiki in 1977, becoming the *Homeric Renaissance*, but a charter to Costa Cruises saw her renamed *World Renaissance*. Sold to Indonesian buyers in 1995, she became the Djakarta-based *Awani Dream*, but then was resold to Epirotiki in 1998 and renamed *World Renaissance*. Sold in 2005, she became the *Grand Victoria*. *(Luis Miguel Correia)*

Opposite, clockwise from top left:
Fleetmates together – the *World Renaissance* and the *Stella Solaris* together at Manaus in Brazil, in January 1987. *(Author's Collection)*

French Line's *Flandre*, completed in 1952 for North Atlantic service between Le Havre and New York, became the Costa cruise ship *Carla 'C'* in 1968, a name restyled as *Carla Costa* in 1986. Sold to Epirotiki in 1992, she became the *Pallas Athena* mostly for seven-day Aegean cruises out of Piraeus. Ruined by a fire in Piraeus, on March 24th 1994, she was quickly declared a complete loss and sold that December to Turkish breakers. *(Antonio Scrimali)*

The cruise ship-ferry *Pegasus* had been the Baltic Sea-based *Svea Corona*, completed in 1975 and then one of the largest ferries afloat. She became the American-owned *Sundancer* in 1984, but barely entered Alaskan cruise service when she went aground and was so damaged as to be declared a total loss. Epirotiki bought her, however, and had her repaired in Greece as the *Pegasus*. Unfortunately, she caught fire at her Venice berth in June 1991 and was scrapped at Aliaga, Turkey in 1994. *(World Ship Society)*

Epirotiki bought Norwegian Cruise Lines' *Sunward II* in 1991 and then renamed the 13,995-tonner as the *Triton*. Built at Rotterdam in 1971, she had been the *Cunard Adventurer* until 1977. *(Luis Miguel Correia)*

NEAR SISTERS: THE OLYMPIC AND THE APOLLON

'It was always rather odd that Potomianos bought these two ships. They were really too old,' noted Arthur Crook when discussing the sales of Carnival Cruise Lines' former *Carnivale* and ex-*Mardi Gras* to Epirotiki Lines. 'He thought that he was getting a good deal. Of course, they had very solid hulls, but really that is all they had. Their machinery was old and tired. Both are, of course, steam turbine. But the Greeks are really the only ones left that still run turbines. There are still steam engineers around. There's no one else really. Greek officers and sailors are also just the only ones left that are prepared to do shipyard work while aboard, even while sailing.'

Both were former Canadian Pacific liners: the *Carnivale* began her days as the Glasgow-built *Empress of Britain* in 1956 and later sailed as Greek Line's *Queen Anna Maria* (1965–75); the *Mardi Gras* had been the *Empress of Canada*, completed at Newcastle in 1961. The 650-foot-long *Empress of Canada* finished Canadian Pacific's liner services altogether in late 1971 and shortly thereafter became the first ship for the Carnival Cruise Lines. She sailed as the *Mardi Gras* until sold to Epirotiki in 1993 and briefly thought to become their *Olympic*, but used instead for gambling cruises out of American ports as the *Star of Texas* and then as the *Lucky Star*. She rejoined Epirotiki's own fleet in 1995 and was renamed *Apollon*. The *Queen Anna Maria* (ex-*Empress of Britain*) joined Carnival in 1975 and was renamed *Carnivale*. She had a short and unsuccessful stint as the *Fiesta Marina* for Spanish-language Caribbean

cruises in 1993, but by May 1994 was in Epirotiki's fleet as the *Olympic*, the name intended for the former *Mardi Gras*. The *Olympic* ran mostly seven-day Aegean cruises out of Piraeus whereas the *Apollon* spent much of her time in lay-up, awaiting a charter.

Captain Evgenios Misailides served aboard the *Olympic* in 1995, when she was running seven-day Aegean cruises out of Piraeus. 'She was then still in good shape considering her long life,' he said. 'The hull was very solid and the engines, piping and plates were good, but she had some difficulties – she had practically no maneuverability. There were no thrusters and only the simplest of gears. She always needed, for example, four tugs at Piraeus. She was also expensive to operate, required more engineers and had a higher fuel consumption. She was laid-up in winter. In November 1997, she went out to Qatar for use for one week as a floating hotel for a worldwide economic conference. She was joined there by the *Triton* and the *Ocean Majesty*. Soon after her return to Greece, she was sold to Paris Katsoufis and renamed *Topaz*. It was rumored at first that she was sold to Far East buyers, but instead remained under Greek ownership.'

The 1,050-berth *Topaz* currently runs around-the-world cruises under charter to the Japanese. Her actual owners are listed, however, as Topaz International Shipping Company.

Clive Harvey, a devoted ocean liner historian and author, made a trip aboard the former *Empress of Britain*. 'Stepping aboard the *Topaz*, it was quite evident that her several different owners had given her the greatest attention and care,' he noted. 'For even in April 1999, forty-four years after she was launched, she

Epirotiki obtained two former Canadian Pacific transatlantic liners in 1994 and 1995. The first, the former *Empress of Britain,* built in 1956, later sailed as Greek Line's *Queen Anna Maria* (1964–75) and then as Carnival Cruise Lines' *Carnivale* (1975–93). She then had a brief stint (1993–94) as the *Fiesta Marina* for a short-lived Carnival subsidiary, Fiesta Cruise Lines. Beginning in 1994, Epirotiki began using the 1,050-berth ship as the *Olympic. (Michael D. J. Lennon)*

Clockwise from top left:

The 640-foot-long ship was sold yet again, in 1997, becoming the *Topaz* for Greek owners, Topaz International Shipping. She has since done mostly charter cruising. *(Michael Cassar)*

Canadian Pacific's last Atlantic liner, the 650-foot *Empress of Canada*, was completed in 1961, but sold by 1972 to become Carnival Cruise Lines' first passenger ship, the *Mardi Gras*. She was sold in 1993, becoming the casino ships *Star of Texas* and later *Lucky Star*. She was renamed *Apollon* in 1997 and used in charter cruising for Epirotiki. *(Clive Harvey)*

Laid up in her in final years, the *Apollon* went to Indian breakers in 2004. *(Clive Harvey)*

The 16,795-ton, 950-passenger *Olympic Countess* joined Epirotiki in 1998. Previously, she had been the *Cunard Countess*. She was sold in 2005, becoming the *Ocean Countess* and then the *Lili Marleen*. *(Author's Collection)*

appeared to be in splendid condition, with all her decks, cabins and public rooms being well maintained. It was unfortunate that much of her 'ocean liner deco' style decor had been removed and replaced with a more modern look of bright colors and reflective surfaces that in places were quite at odds with the still distinctly 1950s feel of the ship. There were, however, some areas where the original features had been retained: some elegant paneling, etched glass panels on brass trimmed doors and heavy brass rails. The somewhat inappropriately named Windjammer Lounge seemed to have more or less escaped all those makeovers, retaining most of its original style and charm. As with any former liner, she has those wonderful small areas of deck on which to sunbathe. Despite the changes made to the *Topaz,* she still retains the feel on an Atlantic liner even if most of her life has been spent as a cruise ship.'

The *Apollon*, after some charter cruising for another British firm, First Choice Cruises, began running short, three- and four-day Aegean cruises in March 2001. Laid-up by 2004, she was soon sold to Indian shipbreakers.

CHAPTER VIII

FESTIVAL CRUISES

Above left: When Festival Cruises began sailings in the Mediterranean in 1994, their Greek parent owners could not have foreseen their great growth. In less than ten years, they had six cruise ships, including three new builds. The 14,717-ton *The Azur* was the first of Festival's ships. She had been built in 1971 as P&O's *Eagle* and then, in 1975, became *Azur* for France's Nouvelle Cie. de Paquebots. Quickly, she was in service, however, for Chandris Cruises as *The Azur*. The 1,039-berth ship is seen here at Funchal, on November 2nd 1989, with P&O's *Canberra* in the background. Auctioned-off in 2004, she became the *Eloise* and then *Royal Iris*. *(Luis Miguel Correia)*

Above right: *The Azur* is seen here at Venice, in July 1998, with the Company's second ship, the 15,781-ton *Bolero* berthed just behind. She had been the *Starward* of Norwegian Cruise Lines, completed in 1968 and sold to Festival in 1995. Auctioned-off in 2004, she was sold to Lebanese buyers. and became the *Orient Queen*. *(Author's Collection)*

Right: The 17,042-ton *Flamenco* joined Festival in 1997. Italian-built in 1972, she had been P&O's *Spirit of London* and then *Sun Princess* for Princess Cruises. In 1989, she became the *Starship Majestic* for Premier Cruise Lines and then, in 1995, had a two-year stint as the *Southern Cross* for CTC Lines. Sold off in 2005, she became the *New Flamenco* for charter to Spain's Globalia. *(Michael Cassar)*

Below left: Great success at Festival led to their first newbuild within five years. The 47,000-ton *Mistral*, built by Chantiers de l'Atlantique at St Nazaire, was added in 1999. *(Philippe Brebant)*

Below right: A great success, the *Mistral* led Festival back to the same French builders for a pair of 58,000-ton sister ships, the *European Vision* and *European Stars*. These ships were added in 2001 and 2002 respectively and were to be followed by a pair of 80,000-ton sisters, also from St Nazaire. Unfortunately, Festival slipped into bankruptcy by early 2004 and their once popular fleet sent off to auction blocks. In 2005, the *Mistral* was auctioned-off, becoming the *New Mistral*, while the *European Vision* and *European Stars* became MSC Cruises' *Armonia* and *Sinfonia*. *(Philippe Brebant)*

CHAPTER IX

GOLDEN SUN CRUISES

Above left: Beginning in the late 1990s, several Greek shipowner-partners formed Golden Sun Cruises, especially for Aegean cruises from Piraeus. There were subsequent winter cruises to the Canary Islands, summers in Scandinavia and, beginning in June 2001, a rather unique series of North American Great Lakes cruises. The Company's largest ship was the 16,495-ton, 845-passenger *Aegean Spirit*, built originally in 1950 as the French *Provence*. She was sold to Costa Line in 1965 and renamed *Enrico 'C'*, a name altered to *Enrico Costa* in 1987. She was sold to another Italian line, Starlauro Cruises, in 1994, renamed *Symphony* and used for Mediterranean as well as winter-season South African cruises. Golden Sun bought her in 2000. The Company collapsed, however, in 2001 and the *Aegean Spirit* was 'arrested' and laid-up. Renamed *Ocean Glory I*, she was later auctioned off and sold to Indian scrappers. The fifty-one-year-old ship was delivered to Alang as the *Classica* in November 2001 and soon demolished. *(Michael D. J. Lennon)*

Above right: The Company's other ships were the *Aegean I*, the former *Aegean Dolphin*, and rebuilt a cargo ship hull, and the *Arcadia*, reconstructed in 1987 after being the Spanish ferry *Vicente Puchol*, completed in 1961. The two ships are seen here at Piraeus in July 1999. *(Author's Collection)*

CHAPTER X

GREEK LINE

Above left: The 16,991-ton *Nea Hellas*, for a time the largest passenger ship under the Greek flag (1939–53), was the first vessel in the Greek Line fleet. She had been Anchor Line's *Tuscania*, completed in 1922. She is seen here entering Naples on one of her Mediterranean-New York voyages. *(Gillespie-Faber Collection)*

Above right: The 7,707-ton, 426-foot-long *Canberra* was another early Greek Line passenger ship. Built on the Clyde in 1913 as the Australian-owned *Canberra*, she was laid-up in 1945. Reportedly sold in 1947 to Chinese buyers, she joined the Greek Line instead and began transatlantic crossings. A coal burner until 1949, she was then converted for oil. She was sold to Dominican Republic owners in 1954, renamed *Espana* and used on the Spain–Caribbean migrant trade. She was broken up in 1959 following 46 years of service. *(Greek Line)*

Left: The *Nea Hellas* was renamed *New York* in 1955 and was sometimes seen in the great gatherings of ocean liners along New York City's West Side piers. In this view, dated July 13th 1956, two ships, the *New York* (left) and Cunard's *Britannic*, are sailing at the very same time. French Line's *Flandre*, Cunard's *Queen Elizabeth* and Furness-Bermuda's *Ocean Monarch* are still at their berths awaiting their departures. The first two are bound for Europe and the other on a cruise. The *New York*, laid-up in 1959, was scrapped in Japan two years later. *(Flying Camera Inc)*

Below left: Another former Australian to join the Greek Line was the 9,424-ton *Katoomba*, also built in 1913. She joined the Greek Line in 1946, but then did a two-year charter to the French Line for the Le Havre–West Indies service. Refitted in 1949, she was renamed *Columbia* and joined Greek Line's transatlantic schedules. Laid-up in 1957, the 466-footer was sold two years later to Japanese scrappers. *(Greek Line)*

Below right: The *Neptunia*, formerly the *Johan De Witt* of the Nederland Line, joined the Greek Line in 1948. Used for Atlantic crossings as well, she grounded near Cobh on November 2nd 1957. Found to be beyond repair, the 10,519-ton ship was sold to Rotterdam shipbreakers. *(Gillespie-Faber Collection)*

THE GOOD-LOOKING OLYMPIA

A pair of tugs hooted and pushed and then hooted again as they maneuvered the 611-foot-long *Caribe I* into her berth at Nassau. A cloud of smoke gushed from her single stack, the mooring lines were cast and soon she would be secure; something of the little dowager sitting near the likes of such youthful beauties as the *Fantasy*, the *Nordic Empress* and the *Westerdam*. Fondly remembered by some strolling passengers along the dockside, I overheard one couple: 'Look, it's the old *Olympia*, our first ship. We went to Bermuda in her in the 1960s. It was so different from today's cruise ships, but she had great spirit and we had great fun!'

'The stories of her actually being an aircraft carrier for the Royal Navy are untrue. She was designed and created as a liner from the start,' said James Wheeler, a naval architect for the Goulandris family, the owners of the Greek Line. 'The *Olympia* was the pride of the fleet from the start. She was the first large liner built for the Greeks and a ship well ahead of her time. I remember that when she was completed, the British public called her "garish". They said that she was too modern, even for 1953.' Wheeler had worked for Cammell Laird, the well known British shipbuilders, from 1947 through 1956 and then joined a company called Maritime Technical Administration, which was owned by the technical manager of the Greek Line. He never actually worked directly with the Greek Line, but very closely to them.

The Greek Line had their *Nea Hellas* on the Piraeus–New York run along with several other, although small and rather elderly ships, such as the *Neptunia, Columbia* and *Canberra*, on other Atlantic services. But they wanted something different, something much better. The Second World War was long over and European travel was steadily increasing along with a renewed burst of westbound immigration headed for North American shores. The Greek Government was supportive as well, wanting a large liner to fly the national colors as a representative. And in the Mediterranean in particular, the American Export Lines had just added their 29,500-ton sisters *Independence* and *Constitution,* and the Italian Line was building the 29,000-ton *Andrea Doria* and *Cristoforo Colombo*. Even the Israelis were coming out with new tonnage – smaller but competitive – such as the 9,900-ton sisterships *Israel* and *Zion*. Greece could not be left out. The Greek Line turned to a yard up in Scotland, Alexander Stephen & Sons, near Glasgow. A single 23,000-tonner was planned.

According to Wheeler: 'Basil Goulandris, the owner of the Greek Line, helped design her, but died before completion. His son John Goulandris took over and followed with the ship's design. It was unusual for a ship of that size to have so many public rooms. They were actually spread about. There was

actually no full deck of public rooms. The main lounge was called the Zebra Room, but this was later considered a great mistake. The decor with all those black stripes was not helpful in rough seas. The ship was well designed as a two-class liner. The first and tourist class sections were very definite with complete separation. The 130 or so passengers in first class almost never knew that there were 1,200 or so in tourist class. The *Olympia* also had some good open-deck arrangements, which was again segregated because of the two classes. They ship also offered some great menus for the 1950s.'

'The *Olympia* was pleasant in many ways and certainly a very good looking ship, but did have some problems,' added Wheeler. 'Being built without stabilizers was a big mistake. Not everyone believed in fin stabilizers in the 1950s. It was well known, for example, that the fin stabilizers on P&O's *Chusan* later fell off. The *Olympia* was not the greatest "sea boat". It was said that she had more storm ropes than any other ship on the Atlantic. Over the years, she encountered some nasty storms. The bridge windows had been smashed and there was lots of flooding.'

The original link to Greece was to have been a close one. The 611-foot-long ship was intended to be the flagship of the entire Greek merchant marine and was to have been named *Frederica*, honoring Queen Frederica, the wife of King Paul. But prior to completion, there were problems with the Government over regulation and taxes. The Goulandris family became impatient and so lost interest. The ship was finished with Liberian registry and was named *Olympia*. 'It was embarrassing,' noted a Chandris Lines captain years later, 'that the largest Greek liner flew the Liberian flag.' Even in her earliest years, she was kept from Greek waters, being assigned to North Atlantic rather than Mediterranean service. Because the Germans had still not returned to Atlantic liner service, the Greeks saw greater potential, especially with the migrant trade to North America, and so the 23-knot *Olympia* was assigned to sail in and out of Bremerhaven, with stops at Southampton and Cherbourg, en route to Halifax and New York. Her actual maiden voyage, in October 1953, was a port-filled affair: Glasgow to New York via Belfast, Liverpool, Southampton, Cherbourg, Cobh and Halifax.

'The *Olympia* started her life with a private cruise over to Dublin from Glasgow with the Goulandris family and their friends aboard,' noted Wheeler. 'Later, she was the first passenger ship to go into the King George V Graving Dock at Southampton with a full load of passengers aboard. She needed some mechanical adjustments. Years later, in 1961, she had other, quite unique repairs. Her main gear wheel was changed at Pier 88 in New York using local shipyard assistance.'

In 1955, the *Olympia* was moved to the Mediterranean, sailing between Piraeus and New York. Goulandris felt that they needed to compete following the opening, in December 1954, by Home Lines of their National Hellenic American Line service. They were using a good-sized ship, the 21,500-ton *Atlantic*, which had been especially renamed *Queen Frederica*. Home Lines was after all a company with very strong Greek links through the Eugenides family. The *Olympia* and the *Queen Frederica* were fierce competitors and all the while it was known that the American Export Lines wanted to expand its liner services to Greece as well as to Israel.

The *Olympia* ran occasional winter cruises from New York, usually two-week trips to the sunny isles of the Caribbean, but also an annual eight-week Grand Mediterranean and Black Sea cruise, limited to a club-like 600 guests, which included the novelty of visiting such Black Sea ports as Odessa, Yalta, Sochi and Varna. The fifty-five-day trip in the early 1960s was priced from $1,300.

Cruise travel specialist John Ferguson had worked for the Cunard Line in their New York headquarters for eleven years until he joined the Greek Line office in 1967. 'The first time I went aboard the *Olympia,* she seemed to be a great contrast to the big Cunarders,' he recalled. 'She had lots of cabins without private facilities and three-berth rooms with two beds, but a sofa berth that was more like a shelf than a bed. She had some good features, however. I liked the little Aegean Club, the first class bar, and the dining was beautiful with polished wood and etched glass. The Taverna was another favorite, especially at night with Greek music playing. The food was always good and the all-Greek crew was very pleasant, very friendly. The *Olympia* always had an air of excitement about her, especially at sailing time. It was what you expected of a true luxury liner.'

'The *Olympia* later offered the first regular cruises "to nowhere" out of New York,' added James Wheeler. These began in 1968 and were usually scheduled for a Friday evening departure, two full days at sea and an early return on Monday morning. Brad Hatry, an avid cruise traveler and former chairman of the World Ship Society's Port of New York Branch, recalled these short, inexpensive jaunts. 'In the early 1970s, I used to visit four Greek passenger ships within twenty-four hours almost every week. They would be at New York's Pier 97, at West 57th Street. There would be the *Queen Anna Maria* (going on a three-day nowhere cruise) and the *Atlantis* (bound for Nassau and Freeport) on Friday nights, sailing at 6.30 and at 9p.m. respectively. On Saturday afternoon, there was the *Olympia* (to Nassau and Freeport) and the *Amerikanis* (to Bermuda). It was fascinating: four ships of tremendous ocean liner history. It was a great treat for one dollar. It took fifty cents to visit two ships each time. I remember, however, that the *Queen Anna Maria* was actually the newest but looked the oldest. Canadian Pacific post-war liners were rather dowdy even when new.'

'I had made my first visit to the *Olympia* in December 1968,' recalled Hatry. 'She still had the two-class configuration and seemed rather dated. I liked her better after her conversion for full-time cruising in 1970. The Mycenean Lounge and the Zebra Room went along with the mainmast and the aft cargo spaces. She was upgraded with facilities in all cabins and shag carpets. Today [2000], she is one of my favorite ships as the *Regal Empress*.'

The *Olympia* also made numerous seven-day cruises to Bermuda. She carried 3,500 passengers on these cruises in a three-month period in 1968 and nearly 5,000 the following year in a similar period. By October 1968, it was announced that the *Olympia* single-handedly generated nearly $25 million to the economy of Bermuda.

'By 1970, we were actually doing more cruises than transatlantic crossings,' noted John Ferguson. 'The Greek Line became well known for their seven-day cruises from New York, either to Bermuda or to Freeport and Nassau. The Company had made a deal with a real estate developer in Freeport and so the ships were routed there more and more. All passengers attended a time-share sales lecture, but it was just about a complete failure. We were also doing more and more "party cruises", those weekends to nowhere. We became known as the "good time ships".'

The *Olympia* had actually been refitted in early 1970 for year-round cruising. Her aft decks were remodeled, the aft mast removed and the berthing rearranged for 1,037 all one class passengers. 'The new decor was less than attractive,' noted Ferguson. 'It was all low-budget. There were brown shag rugs and orange or gold velvet bedspreads. It resembled a cheap hotel.'

Financial troubles were starting for the Greek Line as the cruise business became more competitive and operational costs increased. Even the *Olympia,* once the pride of the Company, grew shabby. 'For her Bermuda cruises, the local Government complained that the ship looked tacky, poorly maintained,' added John Ferguson. 'The Greek Line reacted by painting one side of the ship, the side that faced Hamilton's Front Street!'

It was the oil crisis of 1973–1974 that spelled her end under her original owners. About to start a new series of weekly Greek islands cruises from Piraeus, she had too few bookings. Her operational costs soared and so she was abruptly laid-up. A year later, both she and her last fleetmate, the *Queen Anna Maria*, were bankrupt and 'under arrest'. The 21-knot *Olympia* was laid-up for eight long years, rusting, untouched and lonely. Her original stack would eventually crumble from decay. There was talk that she would become a moored hotel ship for the Sheraton Corporation, but then Commodore Cruise Lines of Miami bought her. Rejuvenated at a Hamburg shipyard, she was back in service, but as the *Caribe I,* in the late summer of 1983.

Above left: The *Olympia* was a modern ship with a series of fine public rooms and accommodations. Here we see the first class entrance hall. *(Norman Knebel Collection)*

Above right: The Mycaenean Room. *(Norman Knebel Collection)*

Below: The Olympia reached New York for the first time on October 29th 1953 and received a fireboat and tug reception. *(Cronican-Arroyo Collection)*

She was quite popular when she ran weekly cruises out of Miami but she remains, of course, a reflection of an earlier time. Once onboard, you travel about through a series of ever-twisting corridors and up-and-down companion ways. The dining room, with its columns and veneers, includes the etched glass that was so common to liners forty years ago. A mural of New York harbor remains at the far end. But there were some more recent changes and improvements. The old, twin-level theater, for example, has been rebuilt as a disco and the former first class pool area, named the Aegean Club, is gone completely. In one lobby, a large, highly detailed model of the ship rested in a glass case. It was thoroughly up-to-date (1993) and showed all the recent changes made to a ship I remember so well – the old *Olympia*.

In May 1993, the *Caribe I* returned to New York, on one- to seven-day cruises, as the *Regal Empress*. At first under charter from Commodore, she was later bought outright by Regal Cruises, a partnership of Liberty Travel and Gogo Tours. Reports that she would go to Sea Escape Cruises in October 1993 for 'day cruises' out of Port Everglades, Florida proved false. She was sold in 2003 to Imperial Majesty Cruise Lines and runs two-day cruises between Port Everglades and Nassau.

Top left and left: The intimate first class dining room. *(Norman Knebel Collection)*

Above middle: A deluxe suite in first class. *(Norman Knebel Collection)*

Top right: The period style of the library. *(Norman Knebel Collection)*

Right: The *Olympia* often featured in newspaper photos of passenger ships along New York's Luxury Liner Row. In this pre-Christmas gathering dated December 22nd 1965, there are (left to right): the *Atlantic* and *Constitution*, American Export Lines; the *United States*, United States Lines; the *Michelangelo*, Italian Line; the *Franconia*, Cunard Line; two Cunard freighters; the *Empress of Canada*, Canadian Pacific Steamships; the *Olympia*; and the *Brasil*, Moore-McCormack Lines. *(Richard K. Morse Collection)*

THE REFITTED ARKADIA

'After the *Monarch of Bermuda* burned at Newcastle on March 24, 1947, there was a plan to make her hull into an aircraft carrier,' said James Wheeler. 'She had burned for several days and was just a hulk in the end. Furness-Bermuda Line lost interest in her and she was declared a total loss. She was just a bit of rubbish really. But it was decided to rebuild her for the pressing Australian immigrant trade. It would cost 1 million, half to be paid by the British Government and half by the Australian Government.' The *Monarch of Bermuda* had been one of the grandest of 1930s ocean liners. Completed in December 1931, the three-stacker, specially designed to resemble the big Atlantic liners, was created especially for the cruise service between New York and Bermuda, a six-day round trip then costing upwards from $50. She

was owned by the Furness-Bermuda Line and was joined, in 1933, by a close-sister, the *Queen of Bermuda*. She became an Allied trooper in November 1939 and served with the British Government for almost eight years. She was to be restored for Bermuda sailings when she caught fire.

Renamed *New Australia* and with a capacity of 1,693 all one class passengers, the rebuilt former *Monarch of Bermuda* was managed for the British Ministry of Transport by the Shaw Savill Line. Her only purpose: to carry low-fare immigrants on the run from Southampton to Fremantle, Melbourne and Sydney via Port Said and Aden. She had been a splendid, three-funnel luxury liner, but was now far from a pretty ship. Only a middle funnel remained, assisted by a bipod mast that acted as a second exhaust, and had cluttered upper decks. She was long and flat. All the public rooms were on one deck.

'She was a "utility ship",' added Wheeler. 'The *New Australia* was so basic.

Above left: Outbound from New York in August 1999, the greatly rebuilt *Regal Empress,* the former *Olympia,* has had the Greek Liner trident added to her Regal Cruises' funnel colors. *(Author's Collection)*

Above right: The 20,259-ton *Arkadia,* used by the Greek Line from 1958 until 1966, had a long, rather low appearance. Having been the three-stacker *Monarch of Bermuda* (built in 1931), she was rebuilt in 1947–1950 as a very basic, quite ordinary passenger ship for the Australian migrant trade. To replace the original three funnels, the large single stack was assisted by a smoke-dispensing dipod mast. *(Greek Line)*

She was white-painted from end to end with sprayed cork on the ceilings. She had the thickest linoleum floors. The Greek Line bought her in 1958 and converted her at Blohm & Voss in Hamburg. She had a dead straight bow that Greek Line modified. Her main purpose was to provide tourist class service to and from Eastern Canada and North European ports. She did provide some first class quarters though, which were done in very modern German style. All of their cabins had private facilities and were located on the Upper Deck along the starboard side. There was a small restaurant and a bar-lounge. We carried lots of officers of the Canadian Armed Forces then stationed in West Germany. Tourist class had lots of six- and eight-berth cabins without washbasins. These were actually quite out-of-date by the late 1950s. Later, we added basins.'

The Greek Line found the *Arkadia* to be a very successful ship. 'Once, I remember that Mr Chandris called Mr Goulandris for help,' recalled James Wheeler. 'Chandris needed to replace his *Brittany* for one voyage and so the *Arkadia* made one nostalgic voyage out to Australia from Southampton. She was full-up on the homeward sailing, Goulandris made a packet and then returned empty. Mr Goulandris actually thought of entering the Australian

trade and later actually discussed joint Chandris-Goulandris services, including a transatlantic business as well. The *Arkadia* spent her winters on very popular two-week cruises to the Canaries and Madeira, sailing from Tilbury and Southampton. So successful, the *Lakonia* was bought to join her, but on a year-round basis.'

The Atlantic service to Canada declined steadily in the early 1960s. Home Lines withdrew in 1963 for example, Canadian Pacific withdrew their *Empress of Britain* a year later and Cunard reacted by converting two of its St Lawrence-routed liners to part-time cruise ships. Greek Line noticed decreases as well. Sailings on the *Arkadia* were reduced and sometimes included added ports to increase passenger loads. She was simply too old to be converted for year-round cruising and so, in November 1966, she was sold to Spanish breakers. She was demolished at Valencia and at just about the same time as her long-ago, near-sister, the *Queen of Bermuda,* was meeting her end up in Scotland.

THE UNFORTUNATE LAKONIA

'She was alive with cockroaches when we took delivery of her in March 1963. First, she needed a very thorough fumigating,' remembered James Wheeler, who designed her alterations after being bought by the Greek Line. He was referring to the 20,000-ton *Johan van Oldenbarnevelt*, built back in 1930 for the Dutch-flag Nederland Line and their service between Amsterdam and the colonial East Indies. After heroic duties in the War as a trooper, she was restored but as a migrant ship on the Australian run and later, in 1959, modernized for around-the-world tourist class service. She was already thirty-three when the Greeks bought her. The intention: mostly two-week cruises from Southampton on a year-round schedule.

'After buying the *Arkadia* in 1957, we were anxious to get another liner, more for cruising than Atlantic service. I did lots of studies and conversion plans on potential liners that were for sale,' said Wheeler. 'I recall looking over the Portugese *Santa Maria*, a big 21,000-tonner, and did an extensive study and plan on her. I also made plans for the *Empress of Scotland*, but which went to the West Germans, and for the *Dunnottar Castle*, which was finally sold to the Incres Line.'

'We took delivery of the *Johan van Oldenbarnevelt* just below the Suez Canal,' Wheeler noted. 'She was dead-heading back to Europe with half crew and half detainees. A few Greek Line crew had already joined her. She was headed for Genoa and a refit at the renowned Mariotti shipyard. She was old and completely wooden. She complied with nothing after the 1929 Safety At Sea Convention. There was absolutely no consideration for fire. She had wonderful public rooms with great woodwork and a gallery overlooking the dining room. I remember that there were pillars with animal heads that were illuminated. The restaurant had oval portholes in solid brass. Operationally, she was a great roller. The sea often came above the portholes. There was a sequence: dark, light, dark, light. But she was a comfortable roller whereas the *Olympia* was an uncomfortable roller.'

'The *Johan van Oldenbarnevelt*, the *JVO* for short, which we renamed *Lakonia* at Genoa, was a very spartan ship in ways,' added Wheeler. 'Greek Line added some first class cabins, about two-dozen in all, which became the very best on the entire ship. Mariotti did those alterations. I used to cruise about once a month on her, making notes and planning changes. We had to make constant repairs and replacements. Some of the cabins, for example, had "shared" bathrooms between them, but the locks didn't always work and so there were lots of surprise encounters! There was a swimming pool forward of the first funnel and another aft. One especially peculiar feature was the open promenade, which had windows on hinges that were attached to the ceilings. There was no air-conditioning except in the main restaurant, but which was really useless. The *Lakonia* was usually like a steambath! She had huge, rather ancient Sulzer diesels and these constantly needed attention. Generally, however, she was a good "sea boat".'

After a few cruises, the *Lakonia* was dry-docked at Southampton for further work, in November 1963. Her 1964 schedule had been posted and was booking well. Primarily, she would make trips down to the Canaries, Madeira, West Africa, and to Spain and Portugal. There were also trips into the Med and one or two up to Scandinavia. But her Greek Line days would prove to be very brief. 'We had a one-month refit in November, mostly for engines repairs,' recalled James Wheeler. 'The Sulzer people came over and we took the time to do some cosmetic work to the passenger areas. On December 19th, she sailed from Southampton on a fully-booked Christmas–New Year cruise to the likes of Tenerife, Las Palmas and Madeira. On the 22nd and 23rd, she was on fire. The fire started in the beauty salon and spread to the forward end of the superstructure. Some lifeboats burned as well. The blaze was aided by a vent trunk, which caused it to spread very quickly. The blaze went straight up. It was suspected that it might even have started with a smoldering cigarette in a trash can in the hair salon. The fire started on the night of the 22nd and the ship was empty by six in the morning of the

Holland's *Johan van Oldenbarnevelt* being refitted at Genoa in 1963 to become the Greek Line cruise ship *Lakonia*. (*Greek Line*)

23rd. She was then just adrift. Some people, passengers and crew alike, had just jumped off. Some used ropes down to the sea. Some lifeboats weren't lowered while others couldn't be. The captain was the last to leave by rope from the stern. There were fantastic heroics plus some horrific wrong-doings! In all, there were 128 casualties. The headlines were worldwide and very damaging. Reporters invaded our Greek Line office in London.'

The thirty-three-year-old *Lakonia* capsized and sank 250 miles west of Gibraltar while empty and under tow on December 29th.

FLAGSHIP: THE QUEEN ANNA MARIA

'I recall going aboard her at Liverpool, where she was laid-up. The year was 1964. Greek Line could not have bought a stronger, more adaptable ship,' noted James Wheeler. He was referring to the 25,500-ton, 1956-built *Empress of Britain* of Canadian Pacific. She had been built for the demands of the North Atlantic, sailing between Liverpool, Greenock, Quebec City and Montreal, and occasional cruising. But within less than a decade, the jets had proved a formidable competitor, most of her passengers were gone and her owners saw her as a money-loser. 'We later sailed her to Genoa, to the Mariotti shipyard, where she would spend several months. She had to be improved and upgraded. The Greek Line needed to better compete on the Mediterranean-New York run, especially as the Italians were adding their new super liners *Michelangelo* and *Raffaello*. Even the Israelis had just added their new flagship, the *Shalom*. The *Empress* was renamed *Queen Anna Maria* and was the great promise for the Greek Line at the time.'

'She was an extremely high quality ship in every way. She was also very solid, having been built for the harsh demands of the Atlantic, even for winter crossings. She later outlived the *Olympia* in Greek Line service,' recalled Wheeler. 'Our major task was to give almost all the cabins private bathroom facilities. The first class cabins were especially superb, many with interconnecting doors. They had polished woodwork and many were named. We also built a new main lounge on the aft end, which was a big job since we eliminated all the aft cargo space in the process.'

She did not impress everyone, however. 'I never had a great feeling for the *Queen Anna Maria*,' said John Ferguson, who worked in the Greek Line's New York office from 1967 until 1975. 'I felt that she never had as much personality as the *Olympia*. The night club at the aft end of the *Queen Anna Maria* was unattractive, for example, and elsewhere much of the dated Canadian Pacific decor lingered. She was also a ship that lacked warmth with

nothing special that set her apart. She was, however, always a hardworking ship. I recall many occasions when she would arrive from the Mediterranean on a Friday morning and then sail that same evening on a three-night cruise to nowhere. She would return on Monday morning and then sail that same afternoon for another crossing to the Med.'

She sailed to Piraeus as the *Queen Anna Maria* for the first time in March 1965. 'She was officially named by the Queen Anne Marie of Greece. It was a very special occasion,' remembered Wheeler. 'All of Piraeus was decorated and there was a wonderful luncheon held aboard with King Constantine and the Queen attending. I was presented to both of them. A month later, the ship sailed for New York. But economies were setting-in at Greek Line. The London offices on Duke Street in the West End closed in November 1966. Everyone moved to Piraeus. It was a long, slow, but inevitable decline. By 1975, the *Queen Anna Maria* would be the last of their ships.'

In her later years, in the late 1960s and early 1970s, the *Queen Anna Maria* had begun to make more and more cruises, soliciting passengers from all levels of the traveling public. Brad Hatry was aboard her for a $95, three-night cruise to nowhere from New York in July 1972. 'She was still very Canadian Pacific on the inside,' he recalled. 'The new nightclub looked like an airport lounge. Our sailing was delayed by a bomb scare and we spent added time at Pier 97. I went to the movies and finally we sailed after midnight. Throughout the cruise, the ship reeked of marijuana smoke. There was also lots of drinking. One passenger was so drunk that he climbed the cargo mast and had to be coaxed down by crew members. The passengers never seemed to sleep. There was noise and laughter and music all the time. It was typical for short, bargain-priced cruises then. On the *Atlantis* of Chandris, the passengers were said to be so rowdy that some of them threw deck chairs over the side!'

'The nowhere cruises in particular were often over-booked,' remembered John Ferguson. 'On sailing day, even at embarkation on the pier, some passengers had to be moved around to different cabins, given refunds and fare reductions. But we never turned away anyone. There always seemed to be a cabin somewhere. It was an especially long day for the office staff, with no extra compensation. We had started at nine that same morning in the office in Lower Manhattan, at 32 Pearl Street. In late afternoon, we would go up to Pier 97 and begin the embarkation process. This lasted until as late as 10.30. We would then go over to the nearby Sheraton Hotel on West 42nd Street and have a drink as we watched the ship sail at 11.00. I used to catch a midnight train home to New Jersey.'

'The Greek Line was slipping more and more by 1973–1974,' according to Ferguson. 'The oil crisis of that time was a major blow. Operational costs became insurmountable. Once the *Olympia* was laid-up, the *Queen Anna*

The 21-knot *Queen Anna Maria* is seen here departing from New York in August 1973. *(Author's Collection)*

Maria sailed solo. One ship was supporting a large staff, both ashore and afloat. It wasn't practical. There was also lots of financial mismanagement, both in the offices and on the ship. Administratively, the younger Goulandris did not have the same keen business sense as his father.'

The end came in January 1975, when the bankrupt Company collapsed and the *Queen Anna Maria* was forced to flee, without passengers, to home waters. 'No one in the office in New York was quite aware of the huge problems in the end,' recalled Ferguson, 'but there had been some rumors. The Chase Manhattan Bank actually gave money to the Greek Line for fuel so that the empty *Queen Anna Maria* could sail to Greece. They held the mortgage on the ship, but had far less legal claim on her in American waters. They wanted her in Greece where the laws were different and gave them far more leverage. The office actually closed on Friday and the ship fled from New York on Saturday afternoon. But no one in the office was told. We returned on the following Monday, but sat about with nothing to do for another week. It was all a mystery. Some thought she might be saved. But there was nothing left of Greek Line. There was no money left whatsoever. We weren't even paid for that last week. All thirty of us lost our jobs. In retrospect, however, the Greek Line was a good working experience. If they had had better management in later years, they might have been a Carnival Cruise Lines, a great success. They had similar ingredients for mass-market cruising.'

In December 1975, after a ten-month lay-up at Perama, the idle *Queen Anna Maria* became Carnival Cruise Lines' second ship, the *Carnivale,* and was assigned to seven-day Caribbean cruising out of Miami. She followed in the successful wake of another former Canadian Pacific liner, the *Empress of Canada*, which became Carnival's first ship, the *Mardi Gras*, in early 1972. Hugely successful at Carnival, the likes of the *Carnivale* were later surpassed by brand new, specialized Carnival cruise ship tonnage. In 1993, she was used for an experimental Carnival service, an all-Spanish speaking cruise division, Fiesta Cruise Lines, and was renamed *Fiesta Marina*. It proved unsuccessful. A year later, in April 1994, she was transferred to Epirotiki Lines in a stock swap deal with Carnival and became the *Olympic* for three-, four- and seven-day Aegean cruises. The original plan had been to rename her *Homeric*. More of her story is told in the section on Epirotiki Lines.

CHAPTER XI

GREEK MISCELLANEOUS

'A Greek shipowner, Mr Angelis, was married to a Guinness heiress and he wanted to run a cruise line,' recalled Arthur Crook. 'He called his company Hellenic International Lines and bought an old American-built ship, the *Yarmouth* [dating from 1927] in 1966, had her refitted in Greece and named it after his wife, the *Elisabeth A*. He also planned to buy the *Commandant Quere* from CGT, the French Line, and convert her for cruising as well as the *Nafsika*. But there were lots of money problems. It was all a failure in the end.' Laid-up from September 1967, the *Elisabeth A*. rusted at her Eleusis Bay moorings. The fifty-two-year-old ship was finally scrapped in 1979. *(Alex Duncan)*

Above: The *Infante Dom Henrique*, a 23,000-tonner completed in 1961, was Portugal's largest liner to date and was used on the Lisbon–Africa run. Laid-up from 1975 until 1987, she was sold to Arcalia Shipping Company, Lisbon-based but using Greek officers and refitted as the *Vasco Da Gama*. Running mostly cruise charters, she is seen here at New York in August 1989. Unsuccessful, however, she became *the Seawind Crown* in 1990 for continuous Caribbean cruises. Later a part of Premier Cruise Lines, she was laid-up in 2000 following that firm's collapse and spent the next several years idle at Barcelona. She was scrapped in 2004. *(Author's Collection)*

Left: Greek tycoon Aristotle Onassis's sumptuous yacht *Christina*, renamed *Christina O*, was restored for charter cruising in 2000. Built as a Canadian frigate in 1943, she was rebuilt at Hamburg in 1955 for Onassis service. The 300-foot-long vessel was one of the most celebrated of her time, carrying royalty, Hollywood stars, politicians and members of the Onassis family. She was laid-up in 1976, given to the Greek Government, but then never used. *(Philippe Brebant)*

CHAPTER XII

HELLENIC MEDITERRANEAN LINES

Above left: The Hellenic Mediterranean Lines was one of the best known inter-Mediterranean passenger lines. They began services just after the Second World War, in 1947, with the 7,527-ton *Cyrenia* (ex-*Maunganui*, built in 1911) and the 4,737-ton *Ionia* (ex-*Digby*, ex-*Dominica*, ex-*Baltrover*, built in 1913) and ran an extensive service between Marseilles, Genoa, Naples, Piraeus, Alexandria, Limassol, Beirut, Port Said and then the reverse. These ships were soon joined by two former Royal Netherlands Steamship Company vessels: the *Oranje Nassau*, which became the *Corinthia*, and the *Stuyvesant*, renamed *Aeolia*. The 367-foot-long *Ionia* survived the longest, being sold and renamed *Ionion* before sinking in 1965. *(Hellenic Mediterranean Lines)*

Above right: The 2,696-ton *Lydia* had been the Australian *Moonta*, built in 1931 and bought by HML in 1955. Typically, she was class-divided on her Mediterranean voyages: fifty-one in first class, 106 tourist class, 123 in dormitories and 180 deck class. She later became a permanently moored floating casino and restaurant in southwestern France. *(Hellenic Mediterranean Lines)*

Above left: While HML dabbled briefly in the overseas migrant trades with the 11,672-ton *Tasmania*, a former wartime aircraft carrier, their next ship for Mediterranean service was the 1,546-ton *Media*, the former freighter *Fasan*, built in 1936, which began Greek service in 1958. She was scrapped in the late 1960s. *(Hellenic Mediterranean Lines)*

Above right: The 3,284-ton *Massalia* also joined the Company in 1958. She had been Fred Olsen's *Bretagne*, completed in 1937. She sailed until the late 1960s and then was broken-up. *(Hellenic Mediterranean Lines)*

Below: The Company added the 6,145-ton Adriatic Sea ferry *Egnatia* in 1960 and three years later acquired the 5,324-ton *Apollonia*, formerly the French *Sidi-Bel-Abbes*, built in 1948 for the Marseilles–North Africa service. The latter endured until scrapped in 1988. *(Hellenic Mediterranean Lines)*

Clockwise from right:

Hellenic Mediterranean entered the all first class cruise trades in 1972 with the 4,591-ton *Aquarius*, notable as the first newly-built Aegean cruise ship to be built in a Greek shipyard. She had quarters for 297 passengers and divided her time – the Mediterranean in summer, the Caribbean in winter. But after Hellenic Mediterranean encountered serious financial difficulties in 1985–86, the 340-foot-long *Aquarius* was sold to Jadrolinija for further cruising as the *Adriana*. Sold again in 1998 to Marina Cruises, she is on long-term charter to France's Plein Cap. *(Author's Collection)*

Similar looking to the *Aquarius*, but more of a ferry, the 5,200-ton *Castalia* was the only other new build for HML and was completed in 1974. After 1986, she changed hands often, however, becoming the *Stena America*, *Scandinavia Saga*, *Pride of San Diego*, *Tropic Star II.*, *Stena Arcadia*, *Emerald Empress*, *Sofia*, *Enchanted Sun*, *Texas Treasure*, *Enchanted Sun*, *The Talisman*, *Manistal* and then *Mirage*. *(Michael Cassar)*

Two well-known North Sea passenger ships, Swedish Lloyd's *Britannia* and *Suecia*, built in 1929 for London–Gothenburg service, joined HML in 1966. They became the *Cynthia* and *Isthmia* respectively. These 4,600-tonners endured until scrapped in 1973 and 1974. *(Gillespie-Faber Collection)*

CHAPTER XIII

HOME LINES

Quietly, just before noon on Sunday, October 2nd 1988, Home Lines' *Atlantic* slipped out of New York – without passengers, unescorted, almost unnoticed – and sailed off to Port Canaveral before beginning a new career. Thereafter, she would sail for Florida's Premier Cruise Lines. Her original owners, the Genoa-based Home Lines, and sold earlier that same year to Seattle-headquartered Holland America Line, was closing up. A few weeks later, the *Homeric* finished service as well, but she stayed with the Dutch, becoming their *Westerdam*. Home Lines was no more.

They were an international creation, developed just after the Second World War and just as thousands of immigrants, displaced persons and refugees needed transport overseas, mostly to places such as South America, North America and Australia for resettlement. Home Lines represented Italian interests, Greek, Swiss, American and, perhaps most notably, Swedish investment from the huge Brostrom Group, the owners of the impeccable Swedish American Line. That connection was best seen in the very similar funnel markings on the Swedish American and Home liners.

Home Lines' first ships were a mixed lot, all second-hand, all ageing, but all capable of being rebuilt with greatly increased capacities. The first in the fleet was the thirty-three-year-old *Bergensfjord* of the Norwegian America Line, which was sent off on the Genoa–East Coast of South America run as the *Argentina* in late 1946. Next, there was the fire-damaged *Kungsholm* of 1928, a 21,500-tonner of pre-war Swedish American fame, which was

repaired and became the *Italia*. The third ship was in fact the oldest on the Atlantic run, another former Swedish American liner, the *Drottningholm* of 1905, which became the *Brasil* and later the *Homeland*. 'Admiral Vetter of the Swedish American Line was on the board of the early Home Lines,' noted Arthur Crook. 'And then there was Vernicos Eugenides, a Greek, and Mario Vespa and Charalambos Kesseugulou as vice presidents. Another Greek, a Mr Samarakis, was also involved. The purchase of the *Drottningholm* and the *Kungsholm* were through Admiral Vetter.'

By 1949, and due to currency problems in Latin America, Home Lines swung their interests to New York and later still to Canada's St Lawrence River area, to Quebec City and Montreal. The first Manhattan arrival took place in May of that year when the Company's next addition, the *Atlantic*, the former Matson liner *Malolo* and later their *Matsonia*, steamed inbound along the Hudson. Later, in 1953, another ex-Matson, the *Mariposa,* joined and became the *Homeric*. For some years afterward, she was the Home Lines' flagship. Arthur Crook added, 'Mr Kesseugulou had a close friend, who was on the board of the Matson Line in San Francisco. This friend instigated the sale of the *Matsonia* and later the *Mariposa* as well to Home Lines, and still later even loaned Kesseugulou the money to start the Sun Line in 1957 and buy his first ship, the *Stella Maris I.*'

In those years, the 1950s, and before the decisive appearance of the jet, Home Lines began to run cruises to the West Indies and mostly from New

York, but only in the winter, off-season months. There were the likes of fifteen days on the *Homeric* for $450 and up. For the rest of the year the Company ran a two-class service (first and tourist) on the North Atlantic: from Northern Europe (Hamburg, Southampton, Le Havre, etc.) and from the Mediterranean (Piraeus, Naples, Gibraltar, etc.). There were further changes, many of them in the years ahead, in fact. While several of the earlier ships were rightfully sold to the breakers or to other owners, the *Atlantic* was transferred over to a new Greek subsidiary, the National Hellenic American Line, and became the *Queen Frederica*. Another affiliate, the Hamburg Atlantic Line, was formed and added the 30,000-ton *Hanseatic,* the onetime *Empress of Japan* and later the *Empress of Scotland* of Canadian Pacific. Perhaps most significantly, the *Italia* was pulled off the Atlantic trade in 1960 (due to declining passenger loads) and then became one of the first liners to run year-round cruises from New York – seven-day round-trips to Nassau, sailing every Saturday afternoon and with fares from $170.

Three years later, in 1963, the *Homeric* closed out the European service from Montreal and turned to full time cruising as well. Even the Company's brand new flagship, due in the spring of 1965, and their first new build, the spectacular 39,000-ton *Oceanic*, was reassigned – from intended transatlantic crossings to weekly jaunts to Nassau. Home Lines' Atlantic service had ended completely after the *Hanseatic* burned at her New York pier in September 1966 and the *Queen Frederica* was sold to the Chandris Lines in 1965.

'The *Galileo Galilei* and *Guglielmo Marconi* of Lloyd Triestino and the *Oceanic* were among the finest passenger ships ever built,' noted Arthur Crook. 'They were true liners, but they were also very functional ships. All three had extra speed because of their advanced hull design, for example. All were designed by a Mr Constanza, who was trained in Austria. Mr Keusseuglou, the mastermind behind the Sun Line, was executive vice president of the Home Lines for Europe in the early 1960s. He was the principal behind building the brilliant *Oceanic*. He did all his own sketches for the ship, even for the mast and the funnel, and then gave them to the naval architects. He even envisioned the magrodome, that retractable glass ceiling that covers the pool and lido area. The actual launch of the *Oceanic* was delayed by one week or so because of a frost in northern Italy and especially cold winds coming from Russia. When completed, Home Lines used British tonnage standards

to publicize the ship at 39,000 tons, but she was really 29,000 tons by Panamanian measurements. There were 200 passengers onboard the maiden voyage from Italy to New York in April 1965. Sadly, Mr Keusseuglou was ousted from Home Lines just weeks before. His great rival, Captain Mario Vespa, another senior vice president, was now dominant.'

The *Oceanic* and the *Homeric* were, for a number of years, an oddly matched, but superbly successful team. The *Oceanic* was said to be the most popular cruise ship in the world, booked up a year in advance and consistently running at 95 per cent occupancy; the *Homeric* was noted as the 'fun ship' for the best times at sea. Their reputation was prized and much envied: rich Italian charm, glorious cooking, and golden touches from the Old World.

In the summer of 1973, the *Homeric* was damaged by fire and later had to be scrapped. There were thoughts of buying Norway's *Bergensfjord* of 1956 or Canadian Pacific's idle *Empress of Canada* or even the American *Constitution*, but these never came to pass. Instead, the *Homeric's* replacement was the *Doric,* then already finishing her second life, having been Israel's *Shalom* (1964–1967) and then Germany's next *Hanseatic*. Also, by then a steady operational formula had evolved: Saturday or Sunday sailings from New York to Nassau and/or Bermuda from April through November; from Port Everglades to the Caribbean for the rest of the year.

Another brand new ship, the 30,000-ton *Atlantic*, was added in April 1982. She was followed, in May 1987, by the even larger, more handsomely decorated, German-built *Homeric*. But these were the last cruise ships in the Home Lines' fleet. Earlier, the *Oceanic* had been sold to Premier Cruise Lines and thereafter sailed in the overnight Florida–Bahamas trade as the *Starship Oceanic* while the *Doric* went to Royal Cruise Lines and became their *Royal Odyssey* (and was later sold again, changing to Regency Cruises' *Regent Sun*).

Home liners were always impeccably white and were capped by yellow and blue funnels bearing blue discs with golden crowns. For several decades, they were familiar sights to me, especially in New York Harbor and especially with their Saturday afternoon sailings. But in this more modern age of mergers and buy-outs and bankruptcies, that wonderful company (and after some forty years) had disappeared. There was a rumor that they might return to cruising with brand new ships, but nothing came of it.

Above left: The first ship in the multi-national Home Lines' fleet was the 10,043-ton *Brasil*, which joined the fleet in 1948 after having been Allan Line's *Virginian*, built in 1905, and later Swedish American's *Drottningholm*. In 1951, she was renamed *Homeland*. Turning fifty in 1955, she was finally handed over to shipbreakers at Trieste. *(Richard Faber Collection)*

Above right: Home Lines also acquired the 1913-built *Bergensfjord* of Norwegian America Line and which sailed as their *Argentina* from 1946 until 1953 (afterward, she sailed as the *Jerusalem* of Zim Lines). Next, the Company bought Matson Line's *Matsonia* (the former *Malolo* of 1927), which became the *Atlantic*. In 1954, she joined Home Lines' subsidiary, the National Hellenic American Line, and became the *Queen Frederica*. *(Alex Duncan)*

Left: The 21,532-ton *Italia* joined the fleet in 1947. She had been the *Kungsholm*, built for the Swedish American Line in 1928 and which served in the Second World War as the USS *John Ericsson*. Used in a variety of services, she ended her days, in 1964–65, as a floating hotel at Freeport in the Bahamas. Proving unsuccessful, she was soon sold to Spanish breakers. *(Home Lines)*

Right: The 24,907-ton *Homeric* had been the Matson liner *Mariposa*, completed in 1932, and a sister to the *Lurline* and *Monterey*, which went on to become the *Ellinis* and *Britanis* of Chandris. A very popular ship that joined Home Lines in 1953, the *Homeric* was damaged by a fire at sea in July 1973 and, considering her great age, she was then sold to scrapping. *(Author's Collection)*

Below left: The brilliant, standard-setting, exceptionally popular *Oceanic*, Home Lines' first new build, is seen arriving in New York's Lower Bay on her maiden voyage in April 1965. She was sold in 1985 and for a time sailed as the *Starship Oceanic* in Florida cruise service. Under her original name, she is currently in Spanish cruise service. *(Port Authority of New York & New Jersey)*

Below right: To replace the fire-damaged *Homeric* in 1973, Home Lines bought the West German *Hanseatic*, a 25,338-ton liner that had been built originally in 1964 as the *Shalom* for Zim Lines. Renamed *Doric*, she was sold in 1981 to Greek owners, Royal Cruise Lines, who renamed her *Royal Odyssey*. In 1989, she became the *Regent Sun* for other Greeks, Regency Cruises, until laid-up in 1995 following that Company's collapse. She sank while en route to Indian scrappers on July 25th 2001. While Home Lines added the brand new, 42,000-ton *Homeric* in 1986, the Company was sold to the Holland America Line in 1988 and disbanded. *(Michael D. J. Lennon)*

CHAPTER XIV

INTERCRUISE

Built in 1952, the French combination passenger-cargo ship *Ferdinand des Lesseps* joined the Greeks, the Efthymiadis Lines, in 1969 and became the *Delphi*. When they collapsed in 1977, she went to a short-lived firm called La Perla Cruises and sailed as the *La Perla*. Intercruise bought her in 1980 and renamed her as *La Palma*. Laid-up in her final years, she was scrapped in 2004. *(Michael D. J. Lennon)*

CHAPTER XV

KARAGEORGIS LINES

Above left: Shipowner Michail A. Karageorgis became interested in large passenger ships in the mid-1970s. He bought four combination passenger-cargo liners from the Ellerman Lines. The 13,400-ton, 1953-built *City of Durban*, which became the *Mediterranean Dolphin*, and the *City of Port Elizabeth*, which changed to *Mediterranean Island*, were soon discarded, however. The *Dolphin* was scrapped almost immediately, in 1974, while the *Island* was laid-up until 1980 and then broken-up as well. *(Richard Faber Collection)*

Above right: The two other sisters were extensively rebuilt: the *City of Exeter* became the large ferry *Mediterranean Sea*, 16,384 tons and accommodating 895 passengers and 350 autos; the *City of York* changed to *Mediterranean Sky*. Used primarily on the Adriatic Sea and in the Aegean, they were also used for periodic cruises, did Libyan charters and even served as an accommodation ship in Cuba. *(Antonio Scrimali)*

These two ships endured for another twenty-five years or so. The *Mediterranean Sea* (ex-*City of Exeter*), renamed *Alice* in her final days, is seen being scrapped at Aliaga in Turkey in July 1999. The *Mediterranean Sky* (ex-*City of York*) sank at her moorings in Eleusis Bay in 2003. *(Selim San)*

Karageorgis bought the celebrated, 23,200-ton *Gripsholm* (built 1957) from the Swedish American Line in 1975 and renamed her *Navarino*. She did extensive cruising before being sold in 1981, going to Scandinavian buyers, but then being nearly lost in a floating dock accident. Later salvaged and repaired, she was to become the Italian *Samantha*, but was finally revived in 1985 as the *Regent Sea* for Regency Cruises. Laid up in 2000, she sank while en route to Indian shipbreakers on July 12th 2001. *(Luis Miguel Correia)*

CHAPTER XVI

KAVOUNIDES-K LINES

Above left: Kavounides began with very small passenger ships in the early 1950s and then graduated to the likes of the 1,940-ton *Philipos*, the former British *Empress Queen*, by 1959 and then to the 3,562-ton *Esperos* in 1962. She had been a German fruit carrier, the *Linz*, and later the British transport *Empire Wansbeck*. Under the Greeks, she ran sailings from Venice to the Greek isles until broken-up in the 1970s. *(Michael D. J. Lennon)*

Above right: The addition of the *Kentavros* in 1965 was soon followed by the 4,500-ton, 1965-built ferry *Adonis*, which was rebuilt for cruising as the *Atlantis*. She burned out, however, while undergoing repairs in March 1983. Declared a complete loss, she was later sold for scrap. *(Antonio Scrimali)*

Above: The 5,500-ton *Galaxy*, also known as *Galaxias*, had been built in 1957 as the Irish Sea passenger ship *Scottish Coast*. Kavounides bought and then rebuilt her in 1969. She was laid-up in 1986 and later scrapped. *(Antonio Scrimali)*

Left: K Lines' largest cruise ship was the 12,400-ton *Constellation*, which was added in 1978, but then sold off in 1986 to become the *Salamis Glory*, a name under which she continues to sail. She had been the *Anna Nery*, built in 1962 for Brazilian owners. *(Author's Collection)*

Top left: As Eastern Mediterranean cruising expanded so did the Kavounides passenger fleet. In 1965, they added, as an example, the converted seaplane tender *Barnegat*, which was rebuilt as the 220-passenger *Kentavros*. She is seen being broken-up in 1981. *(Author's Collection)*

Top right: The 6,200-ton *Orion*, added to the fleet in 1968, became the Company flagship for a time. Built in Italy in 1953, she and her sister, the *Agamemnon*, were built as wartime reparations from the Italians to the Greeks and sailed for Nomikos Lines, then Olympic Cruises and finally Dorian Cruises. After Kavounides pulled out of a greatly declined Mediterranean cruise business in 1986, the *Orion* was laid-up, seemingly finished with her career. In 1995, however, she was sold to Thomas Cruises, a Greek company, and refitted for 'day cruises' as the *Thomas II*. She later joined Epirotiki until scrapped in 2005. *(Michael Cassar)*

CHAPTER XVII

LATSIS LINE

THE LONG-IDLE MARGARITA L.

During a cruise to the North Cape and Norwegian fjords in 1993, a onetime world champion dance team, who had long experience at sea with the likes of Cunard, the Royal Viking Line and others, discussed their many shipboard experiences. They spoke of the ships they had sailed and had anecdotes about each of them, their ports and their passengers. But when asked about their very favorite ship, there was no hesitation. It was the old Union Castle liner *Windsor Castle*. To their tastes, she was the finest passenger ship ever to sail, the quintessential English passenger ship.

The 37,650-ton *Windsor Castle* was built especially for a famous shipping service: the passenger and mail run between England and South Africa. For seventeen years, beginning in August 1960, she sailed in uninterrupted service between Southampton, then a quick stop at either Madeira or Las Palmas, to Cape Town, Port Elizabeth, East London and Durban. At 782 feet in length and with a divided capacity of 239 in luxurious, upper-deck first class and then 591 in more economical tourist class, she was the last flagship of Union Castle, which after its creation in 1900 became to the African trades what Cunard had been to the North Atlantic, and P&O to India and Australia.

Named by the Queen Mother when she was launched at Birkenhead (near Liverpool) in 1959, the 22½-knot *Windsor Castle* glowed and sparkled in what was to be the final heyday of the Union Castle fleet. She was their most popular ship. But gradually, due to shifts to containerized cargo shipping (all the big Castle liners had substantial freight capacities) and finally the defection of even their most loyal passengers to the airlines, the Company that had had eleven liners in the early 1960s was down to two, and a struggling pair they were, by 1977. To tears, a sentimental band and fireboat sprays, the *Windsor* set off from Southampton on her last run to South Africa that fall. Her running-mate, the Cape Town-registered *S. A. Vaal*, the former *Transvaal Castle* of 1961, was being retired as well, but was sold almost immediately to Miami's Carnival Cruise Lines. She was dispatched to Kobe, Japan and rebuilt there for the Caribbean trades as the *Festivale*. Certainly, Carnival engineers also looked over the even larger *Windsor Castle*, but then thought, in whatever wisdom, that two big ships were perhaps too many. Even they were obviously unsure at the time of the phenomenal growth that the American cruise industry would witness in the 1980s and beyond.

And so, the *Windsor Castle* was sold to Greek tanker billionaire John S. Latsis, who had modest passenger ship interests before, but mostly in carrying Moslem pilgrims to and from Mecca. He renamed his latest acquisition *Margarita L.*, in honor of his daughter. But the mighty ex-Castle flagship was used for a far different purpose: she became a permanently moored 'rest and recreation' center for oil crews at Jeddah in Saudi Arabia. In doing so, she joined something of an armada of former passenger ships in Middle Eastern waters in the late 1970s and 1980s. Among others, there was the onetime Italian *Michelangelo* and *Raffaello* serving as military barracks in Iran; Portugal's ex-*Principe Perfeito* was also in Arabian waters as a hotel ship; Grace Line's former *Santa Paula* became the permanently moored *Kuwait Marriott Hotel*; and another Latsis ship, the *Marianna VI*, the former Elder Dempster liner *Aureol*, was also in Saudi Arabian waters.

'John Latsis was a young fisherman in the Red Sea, as the story goes, and supposedly once saved the King of Arabia and his entourage,' explained Arthur Crook. 'As a reward, he was promised all the oil going to Greece as well as to Italy. This pact was later expanded. Latsis literally built Saudi Arabia. He built the cities, the refineries, everything. In return, he later created a large yacht and offered it to the Arabian royals for their pleasure.'

When her task was complete, the *Margarita L.* returned permanently to Greek waters and has been moored in Eleusis Bay ever since. Said to be kept in fine condition, she was offered for sale in later years. In early 2001, however, and just as the ex-*Principe Perfeito* and ex-*Aureol* were being sold to Indian shipbreakers, it was reported that the forty-one-year-old ex-*Windsor Castle* would soon follow in their wake. Indeed, she did – by then the last of the Union-Castle liners – she was broken-up at Alang in 2005.

Top: John S. Latsis and his passenger fleet, sometimes referred to as the Latsis Line, started in 1950 with a pair of small passenger ships. He turned to larger, deep-sea passenger ships in 1959–1960 when he bought two Royal Mail Lines ships, the 14,100-ton sisters *Highland Brigade* and *Highland Princess*. Latsis wanted to enter the booming Europe-Australia migrant trade and renamed the ships as the *Marianna* and *Henrietta* respectively. But plans changed quite quickly: the *Marianna* was resold to the Czechs and became the *Slapy* and then was sold again, going to the Chinese and becoming the *Guang Hua*. The *Henrietta* was promptly renamed *Marianna*, but seemed thereafter to mostly run charters as well as Moslem pilgrim voyages to and from Jeddah. She was scrapped in 1965. *(Michael Cassar)*

Middle: In 1963, Latsis turned to far larger tonnage, especially to use in the Saudi Arabian-linked pilgrim trades. They often sailed from Libyan and Moroccan ports, and were sometimes used as floating hotels for religious pilgrims. He bought P&O's *Strathmore* (23,580 tons, built 1935) and the *Stratheden* (23,732 tons, 1937) and renamed them *Marianna Latsi* and *Henrietta Latsi*. In 1966, for some undisclosed reason, they swapped names — the *Marianna Latsi* became the *Henrietta Latsi* while the *Henrietta Latsi* changed to *Marianna Latsi*. Both were broken-up in Italy in 1969. *(P&O)*

Bottom: Also, in 1963–1964, two previously converted Dutch passenger ships, the *Waterman* (the former *La Grande Victory*) and the *Groote Beer* (ex-*Costa Rica Victory*), became the *Margarita* and *Marianna IV*. They too were used in the pilgrim trades and for charters. Laid-up for some time before going to the breakers, the *Marianna IV* was scrapped in Greece in 1969 and the *Margarita* in Japan in the following year. *(Gillespie-Faber Collection)*

Above left: In 1975, Latsis needed workers' accommodation ships for his refinery and port construction projects in Arabia. He proceeded to buy additional out-of-work liners. The 1951-built, 14,083-ton *Aureol*, formerly on Elder Dempster Lines' Liverpool–West Africa run, became the *Marianna VI*. She was dispatched to Djeddah and later to Rabegh before returning to Greece permanently in August 1989. She went to Indian breakers in 2003. *(Peter Knego Collection)*

Above right: The largest of all the Latsis passenger ships, the 37,640-ton, 1960-built *Windsor Castle*, became Greek owned in 1977. Renamed *Margarita L*, she too was sent to Djeddah. She returned to Greece in June 1991 and laid idle until sold to Indian shipbreakers in 2005. In 1982, Latsis added a third accommodation ship, the 19,393-ton *Marianna 9* (seen on the left), which had been built in 1961 as the Portugese *Principe Perfeito* for the Lisbon–Africa run. Sold in 1976, she became the mid-eastern accommodation ship *Al Hasa*, before being eyed, in 1980, by Sitmar Cruises to be rebuilt as their *Fairsky*. That idea was soon dropped, however, and the ship laid-up as the *Vera*. Under Latsis, she served in Rabegh and at Djeddah, and also as an emergency center for earthquake survivors in Greece. She was laid-up in Eleusis Bay in May 1992 and was scrapped in 2002. *(Antonio Scrimali)*

Below left: The *Marianna 9* is on the outside in this 2001 view, with the larger *Margarita L* behind. *(Philippe Brebant Collection)*

Below right: Among other subsequent smaller passenger ships, the West German cruise ship *Regina Maris* joined Latsis and was rebuilt as a luxury yacht and part-time cruise ship in 1984–1985. Restyled as the *Alexander* and given sumptuous quarters, kings, queens, sultans, presidents and prime ministers have since walked her gleaming decks. *(Antonio Scrimali)*

CHAPTER XVIII

LOUIS CRUISE LINES

A SHIP CALLED EMERALD

I saw her in the summer of 1996 at Barcelona and then again at St Maarten in the Caribbean in the winter of 2001. Whenever ships are greatly rebuilt, their heritage becomes unclear, almost mysterious. I studied her from end to end, from her raked bow to her built-up stern to her partially caged single stack. Named *Emerald*, she was registered in Cyprus. The colorful stripes on her funnel belonged to Thomson Cruises, a major UK air-sea operator. Of course, the mystery was soon uncovered – the 26,431-ton ship was the former American liner *Santa Rosa* and later Regency Cruises' *Regent Rainbow*.

Owned by Louis Cruise Lines and on long-term charter to Thomson, the 584-foot-long ship was built originally in 1958 for the New York-based Grace Line. Then at 15,500 tons, she and a twin sister, the *Santa Paula*, were used in continuous thirteen-day cruise service between New York, Port Everglades in Florida and the Caribbean. Sailing every Friday, usually at five in the afternoon, they were usually routed from New York to Curacao, La Guaira, Aruba, Kingston, Port au Prince and then northward to Port Everglades and finally New York, where arrival was usually early on Thursday mornings. Minimum fare was $595 in the early 1960s for the club-like quarters of a mere 300 all first class passengers.

'They were top-notch ships, perfect in every way,' noted the ocean liner historian Everett Viez, who sailed aboard the 20-knot *Santa Rosa*. 'They were actually quite deluxe. Every passenger cabin was outside and there were a great many suites. They offered fine food in a dining room that was located up on the Promenade Deck and not on a lower deck as on most other passenger ships back then. They also had the novelty of having waitresses in the restaurant.'

But the cost of operating US-flag passenger ships, plus the increasing competition from newer as well as larger foreign liners in the growing American cruise industry of the late 1960s, meant shortened careers for ships such as the *Santa Rosa*. She was laid-up in 1971, idle at a shipyard at Baltimore and later moving about that port from berth to berth. In the end, she was at an unused grain terminal. After more than fifteen years of virtual neglect, she was a sorrowful sight – faded, rusting, partially stripped, a haven only to harbor birds. There had been a string of rumors: revived as a Venezuelan-based cruise ship, rebuilt as a hospital ship for the US Navy, becoming a roving industrial products display ship.

Bought by Greek interests (the Lelakis Group) and said to be renamed *Pacific Sun* (for Coral Cruise Lines) and then *Diamond Sun*, she went to Greece (in December 1989), was rebuilt and reappeared in December 1992 as the 960-passenger *Regent Rainbow*, sailing for the now-defunct, Lelakis-owned Regency Cruises. She sailed the Caribbean out of Tampa, made Alaska cruises from Vancouver and was, at one point, rumored to be headed for New York, but for short, gambling-style cruises out of Brooklyn. Another

Above left: Cyprus-based Louis Cruise Lines has become one of the largest Mediterranean cruise companies. They began in the late 1980s with the likes of such converted ferries as the 9,984-ton *Princesa Cypria*, the former Danish *Prinsesse Margrethe* (1968); the 10,487-ton *Princesa Marissa*, ex-*Finnhansa* (1966); and the 5,026-ton *Princesa Amorosa*, the former *Scottish Coast* and later the *Galaxias* for Kavounides. *(Luis Miguel Correia)*.

Above right: Louis bought *The Victoria* in 1992, a 14,583-ton ship that had been built in 1936 as the *Dunnottar Castle* for Union-Castle's Around Africa service. Rebuilt in 1958–1959 as a modern cruise ship and renamed *Victoria* for the Incres Line, Chandris bought her in 1977 and changed her name slightly to *The Victoria*. Renamed *Princesa Victoria* by Louis, she is seen here at Lisbon in the summer of 1998 while serving as a hotel ship for the local Expo '98 celebrations. She went to Indian breakers in 2004. *(Luis Miguel Correia)*

plan was to sail her from a Staten Island pier. These ideas contrasted with other New York-based cruise ships, which all used the Passenger Ship Terminal along the City's West Side, at West 50th Street. She also made at least two 'Santa Rosa Reunion' cruises with former Grace Line crew and passengers aboard.

The *Rainbow's* original cargo spaces had been gutted and so the superstructure of passenger decks was extended forward. From certain perspectives, she does appear to be top-heavy. Her sense of sheer is also pronounced. She does appear to be very solid, a very strong ship at sea. When Regency Cruises unexpectedly went bankrupt in October 1995, the *Regent Rainbow* was quickly laid-up at a Tampa backwater and was later moved to Freeport, Grand Bahama Island. It was in fact something of a switch for her and another exiled Regency cruise ship – the *Regent Sea*

(ex-*Gripsholm*, ex-*Navarino*) had been at Freeport, but was moved to Tampa. Meanwhile, the *Regent Sun* (ex-*Shalom*, ex-*Hanseatic*, ex-*Doric,* ex-*Royal Odyssey*) which had been in Freeport, was moved to Tampa and later was moved back close to Freeport.

Louis bought the *Rainbow* at auction in 1997 and soon reactivated her as the *Emerald* for a charter to Thomson. In the winter, she was running alternating, seven-day Caribbean itineraries out of Santo Domingo; in summer, she was on varying seven-day trips around the western Mediterranean out of Palma de Majorca. Her 1998 schedules included some cruises out of Southampton, England. By 2001, Thomson was expanding in the highly competitive UK cruise market by attempting to get as many as 25% North American passengers on her cruises. Perhaps a few might even remember her from her Grace Line days.

Above left: Another Louis ship, the 12,263-ton *Sapphire*, had been built in 1967 as the *Italia* and later sailed for Costa. She became the *Ocean Princess* for Ocean Cruise Lines in 1983, but was nearly lost in March 1993 when she went aground and was badly damaged in the Amazon River. Towed to Greece for repairs, however, she was temporarily renamed *Sea Prince* and then reappeared, in 1995, as the *Princesa Oceanica* for Eastern Mediterranean cruising. A year later, she turned to charter service and was renamed *Sapphire*. *(Michael Cassar)*

Above right: Louis added yet another ship, the 13,804-ton French *Mermoz*, in November 1999. Renamed *Serenade*, she had been built originally in 1957 as the *Jean Mermoz*, but was converted for cruising and given a shortened name in 1970. *(Michael Cassar)*

Below left: Yet other acquisitions included the 11,162-ton *Calypso*, a converted ferry built originally in 1967 and which had been the *Canguro Verde, Durr, Ionian Harmony, Sun Fiesta* and *Regent Jewel*. At about the same time, in 1995–1996, Louis added the 960-passenger *Regent Rainbow*. She had been converted for cruising in 1989–1992 in Greece after having been the *Santa Rosa*, a 300-berth passenger-cargo ship which sailed in the New York-Caribbean trade for the Grace Line from 1958 until 1972. She had been laid-up until 1989. *(Antonio Scrimali)*

Below right: Another acquisition was the 12,609-ton *Ausonia*, originally built in 1957 for Italy's Adriatica Line. She joined Louis in 1999. *(Alex Duncan)*

CHAPTER XIX

MED SUN LINE

The 12,614-ton *Atalante* first appeared in 1972 under the Med Sun Lines' houseflag. She had been the French combination passenger-cargo ship *Tahitien*, built in 1952. As successive refits changed her appearance, she did a 1991 charter to Epirotiki as the renamed *Homericus*, but then resumed Med Sun schedules in the following year. In late 1992, she was sold to Louis Cruise Lines. Laid-up in later years, she was scrapped in 2003. *(Author's Collection)*

CHAPTER XX

NATIONAL HELLENIC AMERICAN LINE

THE VETERAN QUEEN FREDERICA

I remember the *Queen Frederica* from a misty summer Saturday morning in 1962. She had arrived at seven, but had to vacate her berth at Pier 97, at West 57th Street, by ten for another incoming liner, the German *Hanseatic*. The Greek liner had to be moved to a unique anchorage in the mid-Hudson, moored off the West 72nd Street Marina. She had to wait until four that afternoon when the likes of the *Queen of Bermuda, Ocean Monarch, Italia* and *Kungsholm* had sailed. New York's 'Luxury Liner Row' was so busy, even in the early 1960s, that berths were often at a premium. But that same day, the *Oslofjord* arrived from Oslo and Copenhagen with a mere sixty-four passengers onboard. The transatlantic trade was busy, but already in decline.

The 21,500-ton *Queen Frederica* was popular, beloved, one of the great Greek liners on the Atlantic. She sailed between Piraeus, other Mediterranean ports and New York in direct competition with Greek Line's *Olympia*. Westbound immigrants in tourist class were a large part of their trade. But there were first class travelers. Charlotte Green was aboard the 582-foot-long *Frederica* in September 1964. 'We were traveling from New York to Piraeus and the trip included a special stop at Barcelona. The entire first class section was filled with Spanish royalties and other aristocrats going to Athens for the royal wedding of Princess Sophia of Greece and Prince Juan Carlos, the future king of Spain. Servants, chauffeurs, even personal hairdressers were put

in tourist class simply because there were not enough first class staterooms available. One American couple in a first class suite was given financial compensation to vacate their quarters, stay in a fine Barcelona hotel and await one of the Italian Line ships that was passing through in a few days.'

The *Queen Frederica* was one of the great, well-built, very spacious American liners so preferred by the Greeks and other Mediterranean shipowners. Strong and sturdy and built of the finest materials, they were ideal for conversion, with greatly increased capacities, and still had long careers ahead of them. The *Frederica* had been designed by the brilliant William Francis Gibbs for Matson Line's California-Hawaii service. She was commissioned in 1927 as the *Malolo*, the first major luxury liner in Hawaiian service, and her subsequent success led to a trio of even larger, grander ships: the *Lurline* (later the Greek *Ellinis*), the *Mariposa* (later Home Lines' *Homeric*) and finally the *Monterey* (which became the Chandris *Britanis*). The four were among the most successful, long-lasting liners ever built. In 1937, the *Malolo* was refitted and modernized, and in the process was renamed *Matsonia*. 'She had been too stiff when built and rolled badly,' added Arthur Crook. 'When she was refitted in 1937–1938, the added weight made her a better sea boat. I believe that in her early days she was known as the "Rolling *Malolo*".'

She served during the Second World War as a trooper and then reopened the Hawaiian service, but only in a partially restored state. In 1948, she was cleared for sale by the US Government to foreign interests, being sold to the multi-national Home Lines, raising the Panamanian flag and being renamed *Atlantic*. She did Atlantic service, both from the Mediterranean and from Northern ports, before being, in December 1954, transferred to a new Home Lines' subsidiary, the National Hellenic American Line for Greek-flag service to New York. She was to be the rival to Greek Line's new *Olympia,* which, to the unhappiness of the Greek Government, was under the Liberian flag. 'Mr Eugenides, one of the founders of the Home Lines, was a great friend to Queen Frederika, the wife of King Paul of Greece,' noted Captain Mario Vespa, a vice president and longtime employee of the Home Lines. 'The royal family was upset as well about the *Olympia* being under the Liberian colors. National Hellenic American was created with the Queen's blessing. It was all a great success, possibly much to the annoyance of the Goulandris people who ran the *Olympia*. The Queen *Frederica* was a huge success, one of the greatest of all for the Home Lines in those days.'

By the early 1960s, however, Home Lines accepted airline domination on the Atlantic and wanted out of trans-ocean service. Instead, they were interested only in cruising, which they intuitively felt had an enormous future. Even the big *Oceanic,* built for the Hamburg–Montreal run, was soon reassigned to year-round cruising, weekly seven-day voyages between New York and Nassau. The *Queen Frederica* endured until 1965, when she was sold to Chandris Lines, who believed there was still some future, if only very seasonally, on the Mediterranean-New York run. Additionally, Chandris wanted a greater entrée to the US travel market, which included future cruise services. The veteran *Frederica* was the ticket. When I traveled in her for a late summer cruise to Bermuda in September 1967, she was actually past her prime. Old piping was leaking and the teak decking needed work and the steam whistles struggled. New safety regulations enacted by the US Coast Guard soon kept her away from American ports and she was reassigned to Southampton–Australia–New Zealand migrant sailings. Still very profitable, she was often booked to every last upper bunk. 'She was a fabulous old lady of the sea. I have pleasant memories, but I am sure that she wasn't really seaworthy any longer,' remembered Gregory Maxwell. 'I emigrated from Australia to Britain aboard her in 1966. It was $130, which included a train ticket from the Southampton Docks up to London. We sailed from Fremantle by way of Colombo, Aden, Port Said and Piraeus. The ship was filled with young Australians traveling the world, returning Greeks who disliked Australia and other Greeks who were going home to bring more Greeks out to Melbourne and Sydney. In those days, these migrants were called the "New Australians". There was still a big need for manual-labor people in Australia in the 1960s.'

The *Queen Frederica* was not only a very popular ship, but one of the best known and beloved of all Greek liners. *(V. H. Young & L. A. Sawyer)*

The ship was nearly lost when, during a positioning trip without passengers from Villefranche to Piraeus on November 4th 1969, there was a fire. At the time, she was some seventy miles south of Piraeus. Repairs were made when the ship was laid-up for the winter.

But even in deepening old age, she had her loyal followers. Captain Dimitrios Chilas spent fifteen years with Chandris Lines, some of them on the then forty-five-year-old *Queen Frederica*. 'She was in many ways the Company's grandest ship. She had Corinthian columns in the lounge, a balcony for an orchestra in the dining room and the general feel of a "real ship". We were running seven-day cruises out of Genoa to western Mediterranean ports under charter to Sun Cruises in the early 1970s.'

Laid-up after the 1973 summer season in the Mediterranean, the *Frederica* spent her final years in that great Greek graveyard of older ships: Perama Bay. It was a sort of 'maritime retirement home'. While there were rumors that she might become a hotel ship in Egypt and later that a film company wanted to use her as a floating prop in scenes for *Raise the Titanic*, she was in fact passed over to local Greek scrappers in 1977. In the midst of demolition, fires were started to burn the old teak off her outer decks. One of the most interesting liners of the 20th century was soon finished-off.

CHAPTER XXI

OLYMPIC CRUISES

The 5,500-ton sister *Achilleus* and *Agamemnon* (seen here being launched at Genoa on February 22nd 1953) were built by the Italian Government and then given to the Greek Government as reparations for the Second World War. They were soon sold to Nomikos Lines for Eastern Mediterranean service and were noted as the largest ships of their day to use the Corinth Canal. In 1958, they were sold to Olympic Cruises, a new cruise firm created by Aristotle Onassis. The 416-foot-long *Achilleus* was also often used as something of a Greek 'royal yacht', but mostly for 'match-making cruises' organized by Queen Frederika of Greece for her three children. The offspring of other European royalties were invited on these rather elaborate trips through the Aegean isles. Clearly, they were quite successful: Frederika's son Constantine later married Princess Anne Marie of Denmark while her daughter Sophia married Prince Juan Carlos of Spain. Onassis pulled out of cruising in 1963, however, and the ships were sold to Dorian Cruises, also Greek. The *Agamemnon* capsized at her Piraeus berth in 1968. Later salvaged, she was laid-up and then scrapped in 1974. The *Achilleus* was sold to Kavounides Shipping Company in 1968 and refitted as their *Orion*. (Gillespie-Faber Collection)

CHAPTER XXII

ORIENT LINE

The 22,080-ton *Marco Polo*, the former Soviet *Alexandr Pushkin* has been very successful in her second career. Bought by the Orient Line in 1991, extensively refitted and introduced in 1994, she has cruised extensively, including voyages to Antarctica. In 2000, she was joined by the *Crown Odyssey*, a 34,242-ton ship built in 1988 and which sailed as the *Norwegian Crown* under the Norwegian Cruise Lines' houseflag for four years beginning in 1996. A third ship, the 37,012-ton *Superstar Aries*, the former *Europa* (1981) and owned by Malaysia's Star Cruises, the parent of Norwegian Cruise Lines as well as the Orient Line, was to join them also, as the *Ocean Voyager*, but this never came to pass. In 2005, the *Marco Polo* continued to operate independently. (Michael D. J. Lennon)

CHAPTER XXIII

REGENCY CRUISES

Regency Cruises, a Greek company with New York headquarters, had no less than six cruise ships in its fleet at the beginning of 1995, and there were reports of a seventh and possibly more on the way. In all, Regency had over 4,000 berths to sell in the Caribbean, Alaska, eastern Canada and in the Mediterranean. But in a year of fierce competition, ferocious discounting and both newer and larger ships coming on line, coupled with Regency's own precarious financial state, it all ended quite suddenly. That October, the Company's Madison Avenue offices in Manhattan closed abruptly and the ships were ordered to nearby ports and to land their passengers. Many travelers even had to find their own way home. The Regency fleet fled, some to lay-up.

Regency, owned by Greece's Lelakis Group, which also had holdings in shipyards, ferries, hotels and real estate, started cruise operations in November 1985. They introduced the 23,200-ton *Regent Sea*. She had been the *Navarino*, and cruised the Mediterranean and South Atlantic waters for another Greek company, Karageorgis Cruises. Before that, she was the celebrated Swedish American liner *Gripsholm*. She had been first commissioned in 1957 and, even into her Regency days, remained an elegant ship.

Success was rather instant. In little more than a year, Regency bought Paquet Cruises' *Rhapsody,* a 24,000-ton vessel that had been Holland America's *Statendam*, also built in 1957. She became the *Regent Star*. Soon afterward, the Company acquired two Swedish containerships and planned to gut them before rebuilding as the passenger-carrying *Regent Sun* and *Regent Moon*. But these plans went astray and instead the pair found their way into the hands of Costa Cruises and became their *Costa Marina* and *Costa Allegra*.

In 1988, the Company bought Royal Cruise Lines' *Royal Odyssey* (ex-*Shalom*, ex-*Hanseatic* ex-*Doric*) and made her over as the *Regent Sun*. Within a few more years – by 1992 – it added the completely rebuilt former Grace Line cruiseship *Santa Rosa*, which became the *Regent Rainbow*. Then, in 1993–1994, Regency added two more ships: the *Regent Spirit* (ex-*Anna Nery*, ex-*Constellation*) and then the *Regent Calypso* (ex-*Canguro Verde*, ex-*Durr*, ex-*Ionian Fantasy*, ex-*Ionian Sea,* ex-*Sun Fiesta*, ex-*Regent Jewel*). The latter operated Regency's first Far East cruises. At the time of the collapse, the Company was about to take delivery of the 22,000-ton *Fair Princess* of Princess Cruises, which was to become the *Regent Isle*. She too had a long history, having been the Cunarder *Carinthia* of 1956 and then Sitmar's *Fairsea*.

And Regency had other projects and plans on their drawing boards. One included the *Regent Sky*, a 30,000-ton ferry hull originally built in 1986 for Stena Line, but sold incomplete to Lelakis and towed to Greece four years later. She was to have been delivered in 1996–1997 as a 1,700-passenger ship, the largest yet in the Regency fleet. But even before, in 1993–1994, there were reports that Regency was interested in operating the 52,000-

Left: The 1957-built *Gripsholm*, which later became the Greek *Navarino* and then the Italian *Samantha*, joined Regency Cruises in 1985 and became their *Regent Sea*. In a gathering of four, older cruise ships at Sitka, Alaska in June 1995, the *Regent Sea* is on the left then the *Rotterdam* (1959), the *Universe* (1953) and the *Sagafjord* (1965). *(Hans Hoffmann)*

Below: Holland America's 24,294-ton *Statendam*, commissioned in 1957, was a popular transatlantic liner and part-time cruise ship. She became Paquet's *Rhapsody* in 1982 and then Regency's *Regent Star* in 1986. Following the collapse of Regency in October 1995, she was laid-up, amidst periodic rumors of revival for other owners. Instead, she was scrapped in India in 2004. *(Author's Collection)*

ton, 1,700-passenger *United States* if she could be resurrected by her then Turkish owners. There were even rumors that she would become the *Regent States* for sailings in the Caribbean. Lelakis also owned the veteran Atlantic passenger ship *Stefan Batory*, the former Holland America *Maasdam* of 1952, which had been in use as a workers' hotel ship at the Company shipyard at Chalkis in Greece. There were rumors that she too might be converted for cruising. Just before the collapse, Regency was also negotiating a lucrative five-year lease for the *Regent Sea*. She would even take on her earlier, well known name of *Gripsholm* for German charter cruising.

By the end of 1995, with the Company closed and its scattered fleet in the hands of banks and other creditors, ships such as the *Regent Sea*, *Regent Sun* and *Regent Star* could only find their way to the breakers.

Above left: In 1988, Regency bought Royal Cruise Lines' 25,300-ton *Royal Odyssey*, which was renamed *Regent Sun*. She had been the Israeli *Shalom*, completed in 1964, and later sailed as the *Hanseatic* and the *Doric*. Laid-up in 1995, she was renamed *Sun* and is seen in this view at Tampa dated 2 June 1997. She sank en route to Indian shipbreakers in July 2001. *(Norman Knebel Collection)*

Above right: Another Regency with a diverse career was the 11,162-ton *Calypso*. The 618-passenger ship had been built originally in 1967 as the *Canguro Verde* and then sailed as the *Durr, Ionian Fantasy, Ionian Sea* and *Sun Fiesta*. She was due in service in 1994 as the *Regent Jewel*, but a charter prompted a quick name change to *Calypso*, a name sometimes restyled as *Regent Calypso*. She was sold to Louis Cruise Lines in 2000. *(Michael Cassar)*

Left: The Lelakis Group, parent of Regency, bought the idle 15,000-ton *Stefan* in 1988. She had been Holland America's *Maasdam* of 1952 and then was bought by the Polish Ocean Lines in 1968 and became the *Stefan Batory*. The Greeks planned to refit her for further cruising, but the project never materialized. In March 2000, she made one final short voyage: over to the scrappers in Aliaga in Turkey. *(Selim San)*

CHAPTER XXIV

ROYAL CRUISE LINES

Thirty-six-year-old Pericles Panagopoulos saw a great future in air-sea cruising when he formed the Greek-flagged, but San Francisco-based Royal Cruise Lines in 1971. The Company soon built the 10,500-ton *Golden Odyssey*, Greece's first brand new cruise ship. That 460-passenger ship, created in Denmark, had her debut three years later. She was designed especially to carry the equivalent of one 747 Jumbo jet load of passengers. Initially, she was used alternately in the Greek islands trade in summer and out of the US West Coast for the remainder of the year. Intimacy blended with fine food and service created immediate popularity and a loyal repeat passenger following. A succession of ships followed in her wake. But by 1996 the Company was a victim of changing finances and the fluctuating cruise trade. Owned in later years by Norway's Kloster Group, parent to the larger, Miami-based Norwegian Cruise Line, Royal Cruise Lines was abruptly closed down in January 1996.

Royal had had an enviable reputation from the start. Their sailings were expanded to Scandinavia, Alaska, Eastern Canada, the Far East and the South Pacific and the Company was guided for many years by a cruise industry genius, the late Richard Revnes. The 25,300-ton *Royal Odyssey* was added in 1982, having been refitted to carry up to 817 passengers. She had been bought from the Home Lines, for whom she had sailed as the *Doric* since 1973, and earlier still as the *Hanseatic* (1967–1973) and Israel's *Shalom* (1964–1967).

In the summer of 1985, Royal announced ambitious plans to build not one but two 40,000-tonners at the Meyer Werft yard in Papenburg, Germany. That same yard was then building the 42,000-ton *Homeric* for Home Lines and was establishing a fine reputation for high quality passenger ships. The order was later reduced to one ship, the *Crown Odyssey*, which was delivered in 1988 (her twin sister was to have been the *Ocean Odyssey*). Soon afterward, the *Royal Odyssey* was sold off, becoming the *Regent Sun* for Regency Cruises, another once popular firm that closed as well, just four months before Royal.

After Kloster bought Royal from the Greeks in 1991, they transferred the *Royal Viking Sea*, a 28,000-ton, 812-passenger ship, that had belonged to their Royal Viking Line subsidiary, over to Royal. She became the *Royal Odyssey*. In 1993, Royal Viking's 212-passenger *Royal Viking Queen*, the deluxe, near-sister to the Seabourn Cruise Line vessels, was also transferred to Royal. She became the *Queen Odyssey*. In 1994, another Royal Viking ship, the *Royal Viking Star*, which had been sailing (since 1991) as the *Westward* for Norwegian Cruise Lines, was transferred over and became the *Star Odyssey*. By 1995, the Company's ships were offering worldwide itineraries. But while the original *Golden Odyssey* was sold off that same year to German buyers, becoming the *Astra II,* there were frequent buy-out rumors involving Royal Cruise Lines itself. Cunard, Crystal and Celebrity were all said to be interested on different occasions. In fact though, there were no serious takers.

Quickly, the last of the Royal Cruise Lines' fleet was disbanded in the winter of 1996. The *Crown Odyssey* went to Norwegian Cruise Lines, becoming the *Norwegian Crown*. The *Royal Odyssey* went to an off-shoot of

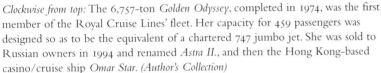

Clockwise from top: The 6,757-ton *Golden Odyssey*, completed in 1974, was the first member of the Royal Cruise Lines' fleet. Her capacity for 459 passengers was designed so as to be the equivalent of a chartered 747 jumbo jet. She was sold to Russian owners in 1994 and renamed *Astra II.*, and then the Hong Kong-based casino/cruise ship *Omar Star*. *(Author's Collection)*

The 34,242-ton *Crown Odyssey*, was Royal's next and only other new build. Completed in 1988, she sailed for Royal until that company was disbanded in 1996 and then became the *Norwegian Crown* for Norwegian Cruise Lines. In 2000, she had a brief stint as the *Crown Odyssey*, but for Orient Line, before reverting back to *Norwegian Crown*. *(Frank Duffy)*

The three sisterships of the Royal Viking Line were among the finest cruise liners afloat in the 1970s and 1980s. But following a buy-out of Royal Viking by Norwegian Cruise Lines in 1990, the 674-foot-long *Royal Viking Star* was transferred to NCL and became their *Westward*. In 1993, she was transferred to an NCL subsidiary, Royal Cruise Lines, and renamed *Star Odyssey*. But when Royal was disbanded in 1996, she was sold to the Fred Olsen Line and renamed *Black Watch*. *(Michael D. J. Lennon)*

Another member of the Royal Viking trio, the 1973-built *Royal Viking Sea* was transferred by NCL to Royal Cruise Lines in 1990 and became the *Royal Odyssey*. In 1996, she was transferred with the NCL fleet to a new, Australian-based subsidiary, the Norwegian Capricorn Lines, and renamed *Norwegian Star*. She later joined Star Cruises before, in 2004, she went to Germany's Phoenix Reisen as the *Albatros*. *(Michael D. J. Lennon)*

Norwegian Cruise Lines, the Norwegian Capricorn Lines, for Australian service as the *Norwegian Star*. The *Queen Odyssey* was sold to Seabourn and renamed *Seabourn Legend*. Finally, the *Star Odyssey* was sold to Norway's Fred Olsen Line for worldwide cruising as the *Black Watch*.

CHAPTER XXV

SUN LINE

Historically, the first local Greek islands cruises onboard a Greek-flag cruise ship, then something of a very rare commodity, cast off in the spring of 1955. Epirotiki's little 1,900-ton *Semiramis* made these inaugural voyages. Success and a promising future were instants. Three years later, the Sun Line, another Greek passenger company, ran their first Aegean pleasure jaunts. It was the beginning of one of the best known, most popular specialty cruise companies anywhere.

The Company's first ship was also small, the 1,900-ton *Stella Maris I*, a former Canadian Navy corvette that had been built in 1944, and then gutted and totally rebuilt in the mid-1950s into a rather luxurious 'cruising yacht'. With space for 125 passengers only, she was used on three- and four-day trips from Piraeus to the likes of Delos and Mykonos, Heraklion and Santorini.

The Sun Line had been formed by Charalambos Keusseoglou, who had worked in earlier years for the Swedish American Line and later for a financially-linked partner of theirs, the Home Lines. He gained invaluable passenger ship experience during the conversion of the former Matson liner *Matsonia* into the *Atlantic* (a ship later renamed *Queen Frederica*) and then with the transformation of another ex-Matson ship, the *Mariposa*, which became the Home Lines' flagship *Homeric*. Dividing his duties between the two companies (and while Home Lines sensibly acted as the North American agents for his new Sun Line), Mr Keusseoglou's busiest and perhaps proudest moments came when he supervised the design of Home

Lines' magnificent 'ship of tomorrow', the 39,200-ton *Oceanic,* which was completed in 1965. There would always be a noticeable similarity in the design and the decorative elements of the Home Lines and the Sun Line cruise ships – in the metallic, Mediterranean-themed artwork, in the use of velour fabrics and in the preference of scoop-style chairs.

The Sun Line added its second ship, the 2,800-ton *Stella Solaris*, in the spring of 1963. She had been built at Hamburg in 1957 as the West German 'day cruiser' *Bunte Kuh*, which made daily excursions to the resort islands of Heligoland and Sylt. Rebuilt at Genoa, where her passenger quarters changed from 1,600 without berths to 241 all first class (and in notably high standard staterooms, all of them with private bathroom facilities, a feature then uncommon to most Mediterranean cruise ships), she inaugurated the Company's seven-day cruises, which included the Greek isles and Istanbul. In winter, she ran two-week Mediterranean cruises out of Naples.

Yet another German coastal passenger ship was bought in 1965. Built at Bremen in 1960 and later rebuilt at Genoa, the former excursion vessel *Bremerhaven* reappeared, also in sleek, luxurious form, as the *Stella Maris II*. The earlier *Stella Maris I* had just been retired and was sold to Canadian interests for use in the Alaskan cruise trade. Unfortunately, she caught fire, burned out and had to be scrapped before ever leaving Mediterranean waters.

Two years later, the Company added a third ship to its fleet, the 5,000-ton *Stella Oceanis*. Barely two years old, she was used briefly as the ferry *Aphrodite* before being extensively refitted for a maximum of 369 cruise passengers. Once again, the Sun Line continued its successful policy for running only 'cruising yachts'. The *Oceanis* was in fact one of three identical sisterships, the others being the *Eros*, which became Epirotiki's *Jason,* and the *Adonis,* which became the *Atlantis* for K Lines-Hellenic Cruises.

'Sun Line rarely advertised in their early days. They had a tremendous repeater business,' noted Arthur Crook. 'They were the top class Greek cruise line. They paid the highest crew wages and consequently had better service and a friendlier staff. They were way ahead of the others. Even when the little *Stella Maris II* ran some St Lawrence River and Great Lakes cruises, the likes of the very rich Firestone family came aboard often. They were regular repeaters.'

Earlier, in 1964, the celebrated Holland America Line acquired a financial interest in the Sun Line. Several years later, the Greek firm expanded to wintertime service in the Caribbean and included some novelty sailings such as cruising along Venezuela's Orinoco River. Their itineraries tended to be more exotic, more extensive, more off-the-beaten-track. As samples, in the winter of 1972, the *Stella Oceanis* ran twenty-one-day cruises from Miami to Cap Haitien, San Juan, St Croix, Dominica, Martinique, La Guaira, Curacao, San Blas, Cristobal, San Andres Island, Santo Tomas de Castilla, Puerto Cortez and Cozumel. At the same time, the *Stella Maris II* ran twenty-one-day trips out of San Juan to St Croix, Saba, St Kitts, Iles des Saintes, Guadeloupe, St Lucia, Barbados, Paramaribo (advertised for 'jungle and river cruising'), Moengo, Trinidad, Tobago, Grenada, St Vincent, Bequia, Dominica, Martinique, Antigua, Nevis, St Barthelemy, St Maarten and St Thomas. Minimum fares for these three-week trips were set at $595.

Prompted more and more by the expansion of European tourism, particularly by airline tour groups from the United States, and the increasing popularity of Greek islands cruising, the Sun Line decided that even larger liners were now required. The sturdy hull and the solid steam engines of the former French combination passenger-cargo liner *Cambodge*, a 13,500-tonner built in 1953 and with accommodations for 347 passengers in three classes, were impressive to Sun Line engineers and designers. Gutted and then lavishly rebuilt, she became the 18,000-ton *Stella Solaris* and with high standard cabins for up to 720 all first class passengers. She was introduced to seven-day Aegean cruising in the spring of 1973, just fifteen years after the debut of the little *Stella Maris I*. Just before, in 1971, the previous *Stella Solaris* was withdrawn and sold off to a Middle Eastern sheik for conversion into one of his private yachts. The new *Solaris*, the Company's flagship, was an instant success. The Company also had an option to buy the *Laos*, a sistership of the former *Cambodge*, but this was never realized.

That ship's good fortunes led to even more ambitious planning. Soon after the commissioning of the *Stella Solaris*, the former Grace Line *Santa Paula* was bought with the intention of also rebuilding her for approximately 700 passengers from her original 300 berths. Unfortunately, this project never quite left the drawing board. Political problems over Cyprus, the threat of war in the Middle East and dramatically increased fuel oil charges (1973–1974) kept the *Santa Paula* at her anchorage in Perama Bay. Some time later, she was transferred to the Marriott Hotel Corporation, which had become a partner in the Sun Line operation in 1971, replacing the Holland America Line interest. Marriott had the ship rebuilt and restyled and then moved to Kuwait, where she served as the floating hotel *Kuwaitt Marriott* (and later the *Ramada Al Salaam*) until bombed and burned out in an Iraqi attack during the Gulf War in February 1991.

The Sun Line continued into the 1980s as a three-ship operation and with a very strong reputation and loyal repeater following (up to 50 per cent by the late 1980s). Alex Keusseoglou, the Company's Vice President based at their Rockefeller Center offices in New York City and the son of the founder (Charalambos Keusseoglou died in May 1984, and thereafter the Line was headed by his widow and two sons), felt that there were several reasons for the Sun Line's great and continued success, especially in the increasingly competitive international cruise industry. 'There are three key ingredients, in my opinion,' he told me in a late afternoon interview. 'Quality of service, quality of product and quality of itineraries. We offer friendly, intimate service. We want passengers to feel at home once onboard our ships. Our hotel staff are largely responsible for this. We are especially proud of their longevity. The average crew member has been with the Sun Line and often with the same ship for fourteen years! Physically, our ships are not huge, but intimate. There is a definite warmth about them. The decor is also a strong point. We haven't gone into trendy or flashy styles, but instead a very rich, very smart, almost timeless look. For itineraries, we've constantly expanded from the classic three-, four- and seven-day Aegean trips to such innovative areas as the Orinoco, Surinam and Amazon Rivers, and to the Panama Canal, Central America, Carnival-in-Rio and around Italy. A special favorite has always been the "Voyage to Antiquity", fourteen days and eighteen ports in the eastern Mediterranean, with all the traditional Greek stops, as well as Turkey. We were the only cruise company, for example, to visit Mount Athos, where only the male passengers were permitted ashore to visit the strictly guarded Greek Orthodox monasteries.'

When Mediterranean cruising dramatically slumped in 1985–1986, the Sun Line expanded to New York cruising, an unexpected area of service for them. To this, Alex Keusseoglou added, 'In April 1986, we made the decision

Left top: One of Sun Line's most popular ships was the *Stella Maris II*, a 3,000-tonner rebuilt in 1965, after having been the West German 'day cruiser' *Bremerhaven*. She was sold in late 1998 to Luxembourg-based interests, becoming the *Viking Bordeaux*, and then became an Indian Ocean cruise ship in 2005. *(Author's Collection)*

Left bottom: The Italian-built ferry *Aphrodite* of 1965 became Sun Line's *Stella Oceanis* in 1967. She is seen here berthed with the *Salamis Glory* at Kusadasi in 1998. In 2004, the *Oceanis* was sold to Indian breakers. *(Author's Collection)*

Right top: The 1953-built, French *Cambodge* was a large combination passenger-cargo ship that was sold to the Sun Line in 1970 and provisionally renamed *Stella* before re-emerging in 1973 as the totally rebuilt *Stella Solaris*. While her owners were restyled as Royal Olympic Cruises in 1995 and later Royal Olympia Cruises, the *Stella Solaris* was sold to Indian breakers in 2004. *(Author's Collection)*

Right bottom: The merger of the Sun Line and Epirotiki Lines that created Royal Olympic Cruises also produced the first new builds for either fleet. Germany's Blohm & Voss Shipyard at Hamburg delivered the 24,500-ton, 840-passenger *Olympic Voyager* in the spring of 2000 and her twin sister, the *Olympic Explorer*, in summer 2001. Among the fastest cruise ships ever built, they could reach speeds of some 30 knots and higher. When Royal Olympic collapsed in 2004, both ships were promptly sold – the *Olympic Voyager* becoming the *Voyager* for Spain's Iberojet Cruises and the *Olympic Explorer* changing to *Explorer* for educational cruising. *(Author's Collection)*

to move the *Stella Solaris* from the Mediterranean to New York in less than a week and then organized a complete cruise program in two weeks. We were somewhat skeptical at first, especially because New York has been traditionally a "big liner" port. But, we felt there was a gap, a wide demand, left over from the earlier years. In many ways, it seemed a natural. We ran on some classic itineraries, to Bermuda, the Caribbean and to eastern Canada. Fortunately, we averaged sixty to seventy per cent of capacity and the resulting comments were both good and encouraging. In 1987, we will run return to New York, but with even more diverse sailings, including several four-day cruises.'

The New York sailings were later discontinued as the Mediterranean and, in particular, the Aegean regained its popularity. By the mid-1990s, however, the worldwide cruise industry had not only increased drastically, but had grown more competitive and fell more and more under the keen, watchful eyes of financial analysts. Merging became a competitive, more effective method of surviving. And so, in 1995, Sun Line merged with a former Mediterranean competitor, the Epirotiki Lines, and the coupling created Royal Olympic Cruises. By 2001, with the *Stella Maris II* having been sold off, only the thirty-six-year-old *Stella Oceanis* and the forty-eight-year-old *Stella Solaris* remained. The latter, rather expectedly suffering from the mechanical infirmities of old age, was reportedly in her final phases of service. Royal Olympic was looking for a replacement for the former *Cambodge* by April 2001. In fact, Royal Olympia was bankrupt within three years and the aged *Stella Solaris* was sold to Indian scrap merchants.

CHAPTER XXVI

TYPALDOS LINES

Above left: Founded in 1932, the Typaldos Lines, which became one of Greece's largest passenger ship owners in the mid-1960s, began with its first passenger vessel, the *Ionian*, in 1948. A year later, the Company bought three out-of-work Canadian Pacific coastal passenger ships, including the 1910-built *Princess Adelaide*, which became the *Angelika*. She remained in Mediterranean service until 1967, by then 57 years old, and was reportedly sold for use as a floating restaurant in South Africa. However this never came to pass and instead she was scrapped at Genoa in 1968. *(Alex Duncan)*

Above right: The *Princess Alice*, built in 1909, became *Aegaeon* for inter-Mediterranean and later cruise service. She was sold to Italian shipbreakers in 1966. *(Alex Duncan)*

Above: By 1955, Typaldos wanted a greater hold in Mediterranean cruising and added the 300-foot-long *Adriatiki*, which had been built in 1943 as a Canadian frigate. She was followed in 1959 by the 2,000-ton *Kriti*, the former British *Melrose Abbey* and still coal-fired. She finished her days at a scrapyard in Greece after the fall of Typaldos in 1968 whereas the *Adriatiki* went more dramatically — she sank at her moorings in Eleusis Bay in January 1968. *(Michael Cassar)*

Top left: Built in 1908 as the *Princess Charlotte*, this ship was a three-stacker that was modernized with one funnel when she joined Typaldos in 1950 as the *Mediterranean*. She was withdrawn in 1964 and later scrapped in Greece. *(Michael Cassar)*

Top right: In 1959, Typaldos looked to reinforce their inter-Mediterranean services and bought the 5,195-ton, Australian *Taroona*, built in 1935. She became the *Hellas* and sailed until 1968. She is seen here in lay-up in the 1970s. *(Antonio Scrimali)*

VINTAGE SISTERS: ATHINAI AND ACROPOLIS

The New York-headquartered Grace Line was once one of the best known firms in cruising. Their *Santa* liners sailed regularly to the Caribbean and along the West Coast of South America. But in the early 1970s, after nearly a century of service and in the face of impossible financial and operational problems, the Grace all but disappeared from the sea lanes. Their remaining ships – freighters mostly – went to the Prudential Lines and were later incorporated into another American shipowner's fleet, the Delta Line. W. R. Grace, the original parent, does however remain in the petrochemicals business. The heirs of the old Grace shipping division could not have imagined that some of their early liners would survive for decades. One, the 1958-built *Santa Rosa*, is still about, cruising as Louis Cruise Lines' *Emerald*. Another, her predecessor, the 1932-commissioned *Santa Rosa* endured for 57 years, until 1989.

That earlier *Santa Rosa*, a 9,100-tonner with space for 280 passengers and lots of freight, was built at the Federal Shipyards at Kearny, New Jersey, practically in the shadows of the New York City skyscrapers and, quite ironically, a facility that lasted until 1989 as well when it was dismantled and converted to a land-filled industrial complex. The *Rosa* was one of four original, identical sisters: the others being the *Santa Paula, Santa Lucia* and *Santa Elena*. The quartet was among America's finest passenger ships, 'little Atlantic liners' as they were sometimes called, and were the creation of William Francis Gibbs, the brilliant designer who went on to design the likes

of the *America* (1940) and the *United States* (1952). There were private baths in every stateroom on the Grace foursome, a roll-back ceiling over the dining room (five courses under the stars!) and the novelty of waitresses. Initially, the ships plied a rather ambitious service: intercoastal from New York to the Caribbean, through the Panama Canal, Mexico and then up to Los Angeles, San Francisco and Seattle.

While the *Lucia* and the *Elena* were sunk during the Second World War, the restored *Rosa* and *Paula* were placed on weekly twelve-day Caribbean cruise service out of New York. Their ports of call were Curacao, La Guaira, Puerto Cabello (also in Venezuela) and Cartagena. In the 1950s, rates began at $400 and there were sailings every Friday at noon from Grace's West 15th Street terminal in Manhattan.

A new *Rosa* and *Paula*, bigger at 20,000 tons and more luxurious with the likes of complete air-conditioning, were commissioned in 1958. But then a rather confusing phase in ocean liner history began. As the new *Rosa* came into service, the old *Paula* was retired first. Consequently, the old *Rosa* had to be renamed *Santa Paula* to run alongside the new *Rosa* for several months. Finally, when the new *Paula* appeared, the older *Santa Paula* (ex-*Santa Rosa*) was laid-up alongside the original *Santa Paula*. Consequently, within a mile's stretch of Hudson River waters, you had two elderly ships, both named *Santa Paula*, and then the comings and goings every other Friday of the new *Santa Paula*. On at least one occasion at the Bethlehem Steel Shipyard in Hoboken, the *Santa Paula* was in for repairs and her overhaul. Not far away were the two veteran sisters and consequently you had three American passenger ships each named *Santa Paula*.

The idle pair were sold in 1961 to what was then the fastest growing passenger ship business in the Mediterranean: the Typaldos Lines. The original *Paula* became the *Acropolis* while the original *Rosa* changed to *Athinai*. They sailed for several years (the eastern Mediterranean and on cruises to Scandinavia, western Europe and West Africa) until December 1966 when Typaldos was ruined and closed down by the Greek Government after one of their ships, the Aegean ferry *Heraklion*, was found to be unsafely loaded after sinking with the loss of 241 passengers and crew. Neither of the old former Grace liners would sail commercially again, but instead went to lonely moorings in Perama Bay. The former *Paula* was discarded in 1972 and scrapped gradually over the next few years.

The *Athinai* (ex-*Santa Rosa*) was left – completely unkept, rusting, all but completely forgotten. In 1978–1979, film makers wanted to use another old Greek liner, the *Queen Frederica*, for deck scenes in the fictional story *Raise the Titanic*. Unfortunately, the *Frederica* was already being scrapped and so the much neglected, rust-covered *Athinai* was selected. The name *Titanic* was even painted across her bow. Towed out to sea for some filming sequences and then taken to the Piraeus Ocean Terminal for others, she later returned to her quiet moorings. Another decade passed before, in a major clean-out by the Greek Government, the *Titanic* was sold to shipbreakers at Aliaga in Turkey. Tugs took the old ship in tow in April 1989 and within weeks the former *Athinai* was finished off.

'They were the best ships in the Typaldos fleet for interior decor,' noted Nick Nomikos, who served aboard both of them. 'It is very interesting to hear that the *Athinai* served as the *Titanic* for a film. But I see some similarities. These ships were from a far different age.'

Opposite left: Along with the addition of many smaller passenger ships, Typaldos expanded with larger vessels and added two American liners in 1961. The 9,237-ton, 1932-built *Santa Rosa* and *Santa Paula*, formerly with the New York-based Grace Line, became the *Athinai* and *Akropolis* respectively. *(Luis Miguel Correia)*

Opposite right: The *Akropolis*, which became a cruise ship, was laid-up in 1968 and then was scrapped in stages, in 1972–1974, with the final pieces gone by 1977; the *Athinai* lingered on long after her sister. Withdrawn as well in 1968, she saw a brief spark of life in 1977–1978 when she portrayed the *Titanic* for a film entitled *Raise the Titanic*. The name *Titanic* was even painted across her bow. She is seen here approaching the scrap yards at Aliaga, Turkey in 1989. *(Selim San)*

Above: As Mediterranean cruise business grew steadily in the 1960s so did the Typaldos fleet. In 1962, the Company bought two laid-up, ex-US Navy seaplane tenders, the USS *Timbalier* and the USS *Shelikof*, and rebuilt them as the *Rodos* and *Mykonos*. Both were laid-up in 1968, with the *Rodos* eventually being scrapped in Turkey in 1987. The *Mykonos* was sold off in 1973, becoming the *Artemis K* and then the *Golden Princess*, before sinking at her moorings in Perama Bay in January 1981. *(Alex Duncan)*

Left: Typaldos added their largest passenger ship, the 13,808-ton *Colombie*, built in 1931 for the French Line, in 1964. She became the *Atlantica*, but was laid-up in 1968 and then partly scrapped in Piraeus in 1970. Her final remains were towed to Barcelona four years later and finished off. *(Alex Duncan)*

Typaldos bought another French passenger ship, the 1949-built *Sidi Okba*, in 1964 and introduced her as the 344-passenger cruise ship *Elektra*. Laid up in 1968, she became the *Princess Sissy* in 1974, but grounded on the Yugoslavian coast in April 1976 and was later scrapped. *(Alex Duncan)*

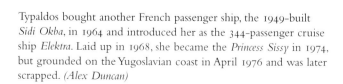

GREEK TRAGEDY: THE HERAKLION

'I was serving on the little *Kriti* when Typaldos Lines' head office in Piraeus called. They desperately needed an extra assistant cook, but for only one night aboard their big passenger ship-ferry *Heraklion*. Mr. Typaldos asked me personally. I would join the *Heraklion* at Piraeus and then return immediately afterward to the *Kriti*,' so recalled Nikitis Nomikos, who had joined Typaldos Lines just two years before. He left Piraeus on the night of December 8th 1966. It was, however, a voyage of disaster – and a voyage of ruination. By the following day, the 10,100-ton *Heraklion* would be sunk, Typaldos Lines would be closed down and Nomikos himself would find himself in an Athens hospital following a long ordeal in the cold Aegean Sea.

The *Heraklion* and her sister, the *Hania,* were two of the prime units in the ever-growing Typaldos fleet of the mid-1960s. They had been British combination passenger-cargo liners, the *Leicestershire* and *Warwickshire* respectively for the Bibby Line. They each carried a club-like seventy-five or so passengers in all one class quarters on the long run between Liverpool and Rangoon via the Suez. Later downgraded to twelve-passenger freighters, they were sold to the Greeks in 1964 and refitted, using their former cargo hatches as garages, with large doors cut along the sides, and were used in the local Greek island services out of Piraeus.

On the night of the great tragedy, a fierce Aegean storm had developed. 'Along with some other crew members, we were playing poker and backgammon in one of the salons when we felt a powerful bump. Trucks in the garage had released and crashed into one of the side loading doors. The door was improperly secured, opened and created a huge exposure to the very rough seas. Quickly, the ship flooded and sank within minutes,' Nomikos recalled. 'Two friends and I jumped off into the sea. I spent twelve hours in the water, hanging onto a piece of wood. Lots of ships eventually came to the site along with Greek Navy and Greek Coast Guard vessels, planes and helicopters. The losses were massive, however. Altogether, there were only twelve to fifteen survivors. At the time of the sinking, there were passengers in the restaurant and others sleeping. All were lost. [Total casualties were placed at 241.] Along with the chief chef, I was rescued and taken to an Athens hospital and then later returned to my island for a long rest. The *Heraklion* disaster made headlines all over the world. It was the worst Greek passenger ship disaster to date and caused great worries about the safety of Greek ships. Typaldos Lines was finished, of course, and their reputation in ruins,' concluded Nomikos, who later joined freighters. But ironically, when he returned briefly to passenger ships in 1977, he was aboard another converted passenger ferry, the *Heleanna* of the Efthymiadis Lines. She burned and then sank, this time in the Adriatic. But once again, quite fortunately, Nikitis Nomikos was saved.

In the major inquiry that followed the *Heraklion* disaster, the Typaldos Lines were found to be at fault. The ship was found to be unsafely loaded and therefore not in compliance with Greek maritime laws and regulations. One of the two controlling Typaldos brothers was even sent to jail and, in the end, the two lived out their days in obscurity and stripped of their holdings. Seized by the National Bank of Greece, little remained of what was once the largest Greek passenger fleet sailing within the Mediterranean.

In June 1970, however, it was reported that the Greek Government had revised its earlier ruling regarding the Typaldos Lines and their blame in the *Heraklion* disasters. Typaldos was then eager to reopen cruise service following extensive overhauls and refurbishing of the *Mykonos, Rodos, Chanea* and *Elektra*. 'After Typaldos Lines ceased operating completely in 1967, the two Typaldos brothers faced ruin in a business sense, but they were still very rich,' according to Captain Apostales Kanaris, who sailed on several Typaldos passenger ships in the 1960s including the converted *Myconos*. 'The Company had a big European following, mostly Germans, French and Swiss, and a few Americans, before the collapse. There were serious plans to regain this by 1970–1971. Spyros Typaldos had fled to West Germany after the shut-down in 1967 while his brother Haralambos went to prison on negligence charges for two and a half years along with a nephew. Later, Spyros returned and made a deal with the Greek Government and the three big ships, the *Atlantica, Athinai* and *Acropolis*, were returned to him. He then sold two of them for scrap, leaving only the *Athinai* for some unexplained reason. He also planned to resume sailings with the ferry *Hania* and at least three cruise ships, the *Elektra, Myconos* and *Rodos*. But this never happened. Instead, the ships were sold off. Once two of Greece's richest and most important passenger ship owners, the Typaldos brothers lived out their later days in virtual obscurity. You could see them, in old age, walking along the streets of Piraeus on occasion. Haralambos was murdered when he was about ninety, in about 1989, by criminals. His body was found dumped in an empty alley. Spyros died a few years later, in the mid-1990s, at the age of 102. They had built a huge fleet, had great, but rapid success and then saw it all collapse. Typaldos was a sort of rags-to-riches-to-rags story!'

By 1965, Typaldos was feeling increased competition from the likes of Efthymiadis with their converted tankers and so bought the 8,900-ton combination liners *Leicestershire* and *Warwickshire* from Britain's Bibby Line. They became the rebuilt ferries *Herakleon* and *Hania* respectively. The tragic sinking of the *Herakleon* in December 1967 ruined Typaldos and led to the collapse of the Company. The *Hania*, laid-up for three years afterward, was sold to Kavounides and renamed *Sirius*. She was scrapped in 1979. *(Alex Duncan)*

The very last passenger ships acquired by Typaldos were the ex-French Line Marseilles–North African sisters *Ville d'Oran* (seen here with Cunard's Caronia at Algiers) in 1965 and *Ville d'Alger* in 1966. They were renamed *Mount Olympos* and *Poseidon* respectively. Both were seized by the Greek Government in 1968 and were scrapped a year later – the *Poseidon* at La Spezia in Italy and the *Mount Olympos* at Trieste. *(Richard Faber Collection)*

CHAPTER XXVII

ULYSSES LINE

CONVERSIONS: ITHACA AND CALYPSO

'The conversion of the cruise ship *Ithaca* took one year,' recalled Hugh Alderton, a naval architect then employed by the Vlassopoulos brothers Nico and John, both Greek shipowners who lived in Britain (and therefore members of that select group such as the Chandris brothers known in shipping circles as 'London Greeks'). Like others, they had owned freighters but wanted to expand to the lucrative passenger ships in the early 1970s.

'They saw a promising future in cruising, especially in the Mediterranean and for the British air-sea market,' added Alderton. 'Their family island was Ithaca and the brothers were prompted to enter cruising by sheer economics. They felt that there were great profits to be made. They formed the Ulysses Line and bought the Portugese *Angra Don Heroismo*, the former Israeli *Zion*, which had been laid-up at Lisbon. She was brought to a Spanish shipyard and converted. It was a major job converting a combination passenger-cargo ship to a modern cruise liner. She was actually a very complicated ship in many ways, one really not well equipped for cruising. Furthermore, her steam turbines were not easy. She had to be almost completely gutted. We put in all new facilities and all new cabins. We were thorough. For example, she was one of the first ships to have her own sewage treatment plant.'

'On the shakedown cruise in April 1973, there were Greek Orthodox priests onboard to give the ship a formal blessing,' Alderton recalled. 'There were many invited guests aboard as well. We stopped at Ithaca and the whole town came out to see us. Thereafter, the ship was given out to charter mostly, to Britain's Thomson Holidays and also to Strand Holidays of Canada. She offered some of the best bargains of that time. Fares started at £49 from Luton Airport, London to Brindisi in Italy and then a seven-day Greek isles cruise or from £79 for fourteen days. The ship was laid-up in winter back then. It wasn't fancy, but it was comfortable. I also recall that we once bought lots of cheap French wine and stored it in the disco on the *Ithaca*. It was later smashed in rough seas and the whole ship smelled of wine for months!'

The Vlassopoulos brothers were very optimistic and soon acquired a second liner, Britain's very popular *Southern Cross*. 'She was laid-up in the River Fal in Cornwall and was available at a very reasonable price,' added Hugh Alderton. 'Fuel oil prices had just rocketed and so it was not an especially good time to sell older passenger ships. The *Southern Cross* was brought to Perama in Greece, renamed *Calypso* and then it took two years for her conversion, from 1973 until 1975. Her first cruise was from Piraeus to the Mediterranean in April 1975. She too was leased to Thomsons. She even made a special, nostalgic Round Africa cruise, but with only 200 British passengers aboard. It was, of course, wonderful for the staff. In 1976, the Company experimented with some New York–Bermuda cruises, filling a gap

The *Calypso*, the former *Southern Cross*, is seen departing from New York in the fall of 1999, but as the *Ocean Breeze* for Dolphin Cruise Lines. *(Luis Miguel Correia)*

left by the old Furness Bermuda Line and later the Cunard lines. The *Calypso* had lots of space, especially in the engine room. She was also a very solid ship. Really, she was only partly converted in 1973–1975. We did the cabins mostly and not very much on the public rooms.'

Actually, Mediterranean cruising was not the huge success that the Vlassopoulos brothers hoped. By 1979, with low returns on their investments, they were looking elsewhere. The *Ithaca* was moved to Florida, to run three- and four-day cruises over to Nassau and Freeport for a new, also Greek-owned company called Dolphin Cruise Lines. She was renamed *Dolphin IV.* 'Peter Bulgarides was brought in by 1979 and saw lots of potential in the US cruise market.' noted Alderton. 'But we had our problems at first. The US Coast Guard actually stopped our maiden cruise. The ship was taken out of service for two weeks. Lots of wiring had to be redone. Dolphin eventually took over the ship and the Vlassopoulos brothers were out, bankrupted by 1982. The *Calypso* was also sold to American interests, the Western Steamship Line, but which used a flag of convenience. She was renamed *Azure Seas* for cruising in the Caribbean, Mexico and to Alaska.'

The *Dolphin IV* was a long-time favorite for short cruises out of Florida. In 1995, she was sold to the Kosmas Group, who created Canaveral Cruise Lines for three- and four-day Bahamas cruises out of Port Canaveral. In the fall of 2000, her US Coast Guard sailing permit was abruptly revoked when it was found that some of her fuel tanks were badly eroded. The forty-four-year-old ship was moved to the Bahamas and laid-up before being sold the following winter to scrappers in India. At first thought to be seeking a replacement, Canaveral Cruise Lines soon ceased operations, joining Premier Cruise Lines and Commodore Cruise Lines in the same four-month period.

The *Calypso*, which had been renamed *Azure Seas* in 1980, spent many years running short cruises out of Los Angeles. Further improved and modernized, she was then sold in 1992 to Dolphin Cruise Lines, renamed *Ocean Breeze* and used on various Caribbean itineraries. In 1999, she was leased to Fort Lauderdale-based Imperial Majesty Cruise Lines to run continuous two-day cruises between Port Everglades and Nassau. Her long, diverse career ended when she was scrapped in Pakistan in 2003.

CHAPTER XXVIII

UNIVERSAL LINE

UNLUCKY SHIP: THE CARIBIA

In the summer of 2000, Andrew Kostantinides passed away. He was in his eighties and living at the time near Orlando in Florida. He was Greek and had been in shipping, but many might ask: Who was Andrew Kostantinides? He certainly has a place in Greek passenger ship history. Back in the late 1960s, he bought from the Cunard Line what had once been one of the most celebrated and standard-setting luxury liners of her day, the *Caronia*. She had been the renowned 'Green Goddess' and was noted for her long, luxurious cruises. She had a clubby tone about her and some of her passengers, usually older ladies, lived aboard for months at a time. In fact, the all-time record-holder for cruising, Miss Clara MacBeth, lived onboard the 34,100-ton ship for fourteen years! Kostantinides bought the ship when Cunard, faced with jet competition, mounting operational costs and therefore huge losses, was quickly downsizing in 1967–1968. The 715-foot-long *Caronia,* always expensive to operate and always more the prestige piece than money-maker, was on the disposal list.

Kostantinides formed the Universal Line, a Greek outfit using a Panama flag and one with high hopes of running seven- and fourteen-day cruises out of New York with the ex-*Caronia*, renamed *Caribia*. Kostantinides was the owner as well as the most visible member of the new company. 'There were secret partners in Universal and these included Cunard itself as well as the Chandris Lines,' according to Arthur Crook, who was contracted to assist in the conversion of the 1948-built liner. 'But Kostantinides was the front man, the so-called owner. His whole family was actually connected with the *Caribia*. There was also Portugese money involved.'

After being laid-up at Southampton for a time and with a rumored sale to Yugoslavian interests known as Dumas Turist (who were said to want the ship for use as a floating hotel along the Dalmatian Coast), the 930-passenger *Caronia* was finally sold to Universal and set off for Piraeus, and finally some refitting and repairs at Perama. The once familiar exterior shades of green disappeared when the hull and the upper decks were painted over in white. The large single stack, once the largest afloat, was also redone in white, but with a blue band at the top.

'The *Caronia-Caribia* had the underwater body of a battleship. She was very strong and very heavy,' added Crook. 'But she also had turbine problems. Once, in her Cunard days, she had to sail empty because of so much vibration caused by the machinery. Mr Kostantinides took a great personal interest in the ship and her rejuvenation, and used to come over to Perama every day from Piraeus. He arrived on water skis and boarded the ship by ladder.'

In the fall of 1968, the 22-knot *Caribia* set off for Naples, but her troubles were only just beginning. 'There were at least two fires between Piraeus and Naples. One blaze was in the funnel,' said Crook, who was aboard at the time. 'The initial crew was a mix of Greeks, Turks, Italians and three Brits, and all of them hated each other. The Turks brought on live sheep at Piraeus and used them for slaughter. Later, the scuppers were filled with discarded bones. We arrived in Naples with a list and stayed there for weeks for further repairs. The boilers needed to be re-tubed among other pressing problems. I remember lots of crew parties using the last of the Cunard wines.'

In January 1969, the *Caribia* started cruising out of New York to the sunny Caribbean, but her posted schedules were short-lived, in fact very short-lived. On the second trip, while off Martinique, there was a serious engine room explosion and subsequent breakdown. The passengers had to be flown home and the ship towed back to New York. She languished about the harbor. She was at the Todd shipyard in Brooklyn's Erie Basin, then at the nearby Bush Terminal, at anchor in the Lower Bay, laid up between Piers 84 and 86, and finally moored at Pier 56, coincidentally a former Cunard terminal (until 1950), located at the foot of West 14th Street. She was reported to be for sale. Among others, both the Chandris and Lauro lines were said to want her for further service. Kostantinides himself hinted at further service, but on reduced, cheaply-priced three- and four-day cruises. But as more and more time passed, the once impeccable ship slipped into irretrievable decay. On a bitterly cold day in February 1974, with little hope in sight and with creditors of all sorts pressing for payment, she was opened to the general public for a special sale: an auction of her fittings, from furniture to china, from wood panels to kitchen pots. Everything was tagged except the remains of the dead rats that could be seen in otherwise darkened pantries and back stairwells. Hundreds bought items, often at very reasonable prices, and one couple bought enough to start a trendy, Deco-style restaurant on lower Fifth Avenue in Greenwich Village. 'Kostantinides had run out of money and, in 1973–1974, he even sold off the remaining fuel in the ship's tanks,' added Arthur Crook. 'He even tried to sell the water ballast at $100 a ton!'

In the summer of 1974, under the guidance of a sturdy ocean-going tug, the rust-stained *Caribia* set off for the Far East, for Taiwan and the scrappers. But her woes continued. During a fierce storm, she was thrown onto a breakwater at Guam and broke in three pieces. Her remains, declared a menace by the US Coast Guard, were soon cut-up and hauled away.'

I spoke with Andrew Kostantinides by phone in the summer of 1999. He was quite pleasant and agreed to an interview. Alas, however, other projects got in the way. Time passed too quickly and a further chat never took place. I wonder what other facts, notations and insights he might have provided and perhaps 'rewritten' on the story of the former *Caronia*.

Above: The legendary *Caronia*, Cunard's 'Green Goddes', seen here at Aden in the 1950s. *(Cronican-Arroyo Collection)*

Below: The *Caribia* arriving in New York's Upper Bay in January 1969. *(Author's Collection)*

BIBLIOGRAPHY

Bonsor, N.R.P., *North Atlantic Seaway* (Prescot, Lancashire: T. Stephenson & Sons Ltd, 1955).

Cooke, Anthony, *Emigrant Ships* (London: Carmania Press Ltd, 1992).

Crowdy, Michael & O'Donoghue, Kevin (editors), *Marine News* (Kendal, Cumbria: World Ship Society, 1964–2005).

Devol, George & Cassidy, Thomas E. (editors), *Ocean & Cruise News* (Stamford, Connecticut: World Ocean & Cruise Society, 1980–2005).

Dunn, Laurence, *Passenger Liners* (Southampton: Adlard Coles Ltd, 1961).

Dunn, Laurence, *Passenger Liners* (revised edition) (Southampton: Adlard Coles Ltd, 1965).

Durand, Jean-Francois, *Cruise Ships Around the World* (Nantes, France: Marine Editions, 1997).

Eisele, Peter & Rau, William (editors), *Steamboat Bill* (Providence, Rhode Island: Steamship Historical Society of America Inc., 1964–200L).

Kludas, Arnold, *Die grossen Passagierschiffe der Welt* (Hamburg: Koehlers Verlagsgesellschaft mbH, 1997).

Kludas, Arnold, *Great Passenger Ships of the World, Volumes 1–5* (Cambridge, England: Patrick Stephens Ltd, 1972–1976).

Kludas, Arnold, *Great Passenger Ships of the World, Volume 6* (Cambridge, England: Patrick Stephens Ltd, 1986).

Kludas, Arnold, *Great Passenger Ships of the World Today* (Sparkford, England: Patrick Stephens Ltd, 1992).

Haws, Duncan, *Merchant Fleets: Cunard Line* (Hereford, England: TCL Publications, 1987).

Hornsby, David, *Ocean Ship* (Shepperton, England: Ian Allan Ltd, 2000).

Miller, William H., *The Cruiseships* (London: Conway Maritime Press Ltd, 1988).

Miller, William H., *The Last Atlantic Liners* (London: Conway Maritime Press Ltd, 1985).

Miller, William H., *The Last Blue Water Liners* (London: Conway Maritime Press Ltd, 1986).

Miller, William H., *Pictorial Encyclopedia of Ocean Liner, 1860–1994* (Mineola, New York: Dover Publications Inc., 1995).

Miller, William H., *Transatlantic Liners 1945–1980* (Newton Abbot, Devon: David & Charles Ltd. 1981).

Miller, William H., *Passenger Liners American Style* (London: Carmania Press Ltd, 1999).

Miller, William H., *Passenger Liners French Style* (London: Carmania Press Ltd, 2000).

Tzamtzis, A. I., *The Greek Ocean Liners 1907–1977* (Alimos, Greece: Militos Editions, 1998).

Worker, Colin, *The World's Passenger Ships* (London: Ian Allan Ltd, 1967).